Contents

Other Books in Series	v
A Great Offer	vii
Introduction	xi
1. Learn About Depression	1
2. Talk to Someone	5
3. Keep a Journal	11
4. Psychotherapy	19
5. Set Goals	35
6. Identify Issues That Contribute to Depression	41
7. Practice Mindfulness	45
8. Connect the Body and Mind	49
9. Exercise	67
10. Eat a Balanced Diet	71
11. Avoid Alcohol and Recreational Drugs	77
12. Spend Time Relaxing	81
13. Get Enough Sleep	89
Conclusion	93
References	95
About the Author	101
More Books by Monique Joiner Siedlak	103
Last Chance	105
Thank You!	107

Personal Growth and Development

GET A HANDLE ON DEPRESSION
Beating Depression One Day At A Time

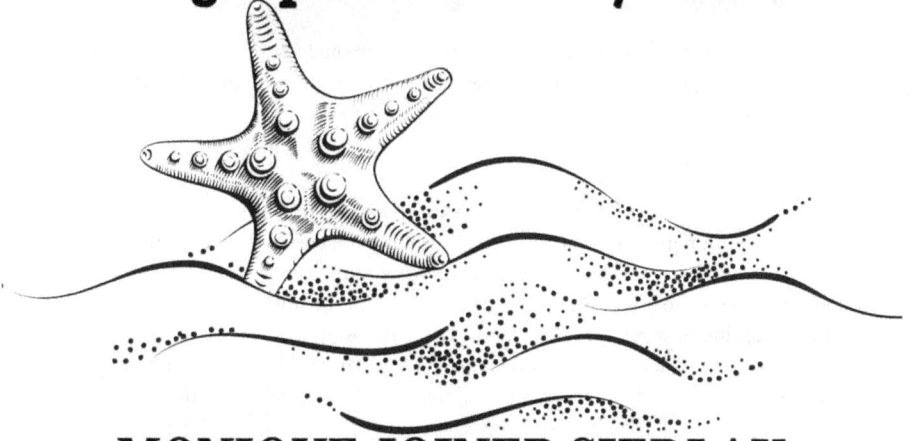

MONIQUE JOINER SIEDLAK

Oshun Publications

Get A Handle on Depression © Copyright 2020 by Monique Joiner Siedlak

ISBN: 978-1-950378-55-5

All rights reserved

The content contained within this book may not be reproduced, duplicated or transmitted without direct written permission from the author or the publisher.

Under no circumstances will any blame or legal responsibility be held against the publisher, or author, for any damages, reparation, or monetary loss due to the information contained within this book, either directly or indirectly.

Legal Notice

This book is copyright protected. It is only for personal use. You cannot amend, distribute, sell, use, quote or paraphrase any part, or the content within this book, without the consent of the author or publisher.

Disclaimer Notice

Please note the information contained within this document is for educational and entertainment purposes only. All effort has been executed to present accurate, up to date, reliable, complete information. No warranties of any kind are declared or implied. Readers acknowledge that the author is not engaged in the rendering of legal, financial, medical or professional advice. The content within this book has been derived from various sources. Please consult a licensed professional before attempting any techniques outlined in this book.

By reading this document, the reader agrees that under no circumstances is the author responsible for any losses, direct or indirect, that are incurred as a result of the use of the information contained within this document, including, but not limited to, errors, omissions, or inaccuracies.

Cover Design by MJS

Cover Images by dashek @depositphotos.com

Published by Oshun Publications

www.oshunpublications.com

Other Books in Series

Personal and Self Development
Creative Visualization
Astral Projection for Beginners
Meditation for Beginners
Reiki for Beginners
Manifesting With the Law of Attraction
Stress Management
Time Bound
Healing Animals with Reiki
Being an Empath Today
Get A Handle on Anxiety

Want to learn about African Magic, Wicca, or even Reiki while cleaning your home, exercising, or driving to work? I know it's tough these days to simply find the time to relax and curl up with a good book. This is why I'm delighted to share that I have books available in audiobook format.

Best of all, you can get the audiobook version of this book or any other book by me for free as part of a 30-day Audible trial.

Members get free audiobooks every month and exclusive discounts. It's an excellent way to explore and determine if audiobook learning works for you.

If you're not satisfied, you can cancel anytime within the

trial period. You won't be charged, and you can still keep your book. To choose your free audiobook, visit:

www.mojosiedlak.com/free-audiobooks

WANT TO BE FIRST TO KNOW?!

JOIN MY NEWSLETTER!
MOJOSIEDLAK.COM/SELF-HELP-AND-YOGA-NEWSLETTER

Introduction

Depression is the side effect we experience when we can't deal with life. Since it is filled with all too many challenges, it's necessary to realize that it was never supposed to be easy. If you are labeled depressed by society, a doctor, or even have a hunch that you are, you should know that it's okay, too, if you are living with depression. It is normal.

Seriously, you are not alone. Millions of individuals suffer from depression in the United States alone, not to mention other related mental illness disorders like anxiety—a disorder known for being combined with depression. It can occur for many reasons, and anybody can experience it. At some point in time, everyone is likely to experience some degree thereof or feelings related to it. People who experience it often forget that they are not the only ones battling it. And since it is not a topic highlighted as much as it should be in our society today, the belief that it is a lonely and individual problem gets fueled by the lack of attention around it.

Imagine if depression was normalized as a topic for discussion in school or addressed by parents to their children. The world would look a lot different for children and teenagers growing up, especially in the U.S., where the silence of suffering from depression and mental disorders has led to horrific events. Just one of these events includes school shootings, which have never occurred as much as it does in schools throughout America in the past few years, with one school shooting occurring every 77 days from 2015 to 2018. These shootings happened at the hands of other adolescents or adults suffering from some type of mental illness, including depression. Anybody who says that mental illness is not a problem that needs to be addressed is wrong. It should also not only be talked about among different age groups but also be taught how to deal with constructively (Melgar L., 2019).

Suppose you've ever learned or been informed about the topic of wellness. In that event, you will recognize that you cannot be mentally or emotionally unwell or feel impaired and be at your best health simultaneously. You can still maintain your physical health by incorporating good nutrition and fitness into your daily life. Still, wellness is not just about the state of your physical being. It's much more than that, and without complete health, you cannot live your best life.

People who suffer from depression are not concerned with their health. They are very focused on their emotionality's negative reality and don't consider their problems worth talking about.

Without mental and emotional health, physical health can be disrupted because sufferers are prone to neglect their well-being. When a person does not care about how they look, feel, and appear to be negative or even unmotivated to improve any aspect of their life, it's a sure thing that they are indeed depressed.

Someone with a healthy perspective about life is motivated to improve, whether it's their health, physical appearance, skills, career, goals, and even build new and maintain existing relationships. Such a person wants to do things and put in the effort to become the best version of themselves. People who do not want this for themselves suffer from some level of

Introduction

depression that should be addressed. As a result of the topic's avoidance in society or portrayed as a weakness, which is also taught and instilled into the younger generations or specific types of people, many will never admit they have a problem. It is usually because of the presence of beliefs associated with shame.

However, highlighting mental illness and being honest with yourself and those around you about your state of well-being—mentally, emotionally, even physically—makes you brave. Although it takes a lot of spirit to admit to it and accept it, you can't improve mental illness or fight depression without doing just that. By remaining silent, you are only disrupting your health further because you are hiding from the world, especially those closest to you and care about you. By accepting it, you can address it, no matter what stage of depression you have because there are countless ways you can fight it. Apart from the things you can do for yourself to feel better and recover from it or learn how to live with it, there are also professionals ready to assist you on your journey to help you fight it.

One thing you should remain aware of and never lose sight of is that you are never alone in any feeling or circumstance your mind has manipulated you to believe you are. If you assume you are, it's because you are stuck in your mind. There are many people around you or even strangers that can, and are more than willing to help you. Since depression and other mental illnesses are internal battles, whether mild or extreme, it's important to remember that we can overcome it. But we must first allow it. In the end, it's really up to us to stand up for ourselves and commence the fight.

ONE

Learn About Depression

MOST PEOPLE ARE LIKELY TO FEEL SAD, EMOTIONAL, OR depressed on some days. Some of which experience it every day while others experience it now and again. Since sadness is one of the six primary and universally experienced emotions, it's necessary to normalize that it is normal to feel it. It should not be perceived as an emotion that is less worthy of feeling or expressing because it appears altering or negative. When you feel intense sadness connected to feeling hopeless, helpless, and even worthless, it is a sign that you could have clinical depression. A condition that is treatable with prescribed medication.

It's a great relief to know that depression can be treated with the right medication and necessary help. Still, first, you have to identify it, which can't only be done by considering the intensity of the sadness you feel.

How Sadness Intensity Can Be Identified

Consistent Negativity

Feeling negative or sad most of the day, particularly in the morning when even the idea of a new day gets you down.

How you begin your day sets the mood of your day. If your morning mood is sadness, your entire day will likely be filled with this mood.

Feeling Too Tired

Feeling fatigued or lacking the energy to fulfill tasks or doing things you like to do. A good example of feeling like this can be not wanting to get out of bed or get dressed in the morning as you don't feel much promise to take on the day in a positive spirit. When caused by a lack of sleep, suffering from insomnia, or oversleeping, could indicate that you would rather spend your day sleeping than joining the world on a new day.

Lacking Self-Feelings

Constant or recurring emotions of guilt, dissatisfaction, or worthlessness daily. Not practicing self-care is another symptom of lacking self-worth, self-respect, and self-love.

Inability to Focus, Make Decisions, Or Recall Details

Feeling like you want to avoid people or not engage in life is a big red flag to feeling depressed because you don't feel like you are a part of something. Disconnection from people especially can make you feel lower than you could ever imagine.

Thoughts About Self-Harm

The contemplation or idea of suicide, death, or self-harm is present in your life indicates that your depression has got to the point that you need to seek help. When you reach this point, you can no longer try to take care of it yourself. You have to seek professional help.

Weight-Loss or Weight-Gain

It can be indicated by losing your appetite or feeling like you need to eat certain foods or overeat to feel better. A depressed individual is more likely to not look after themselves, especially how they look or take care of their personal hygiene or appearance.

Restlessness

Feeling like you are supposed to do something else can indicate some depression, accompanied by fear of resentment. When you feel restless, you are doing something that goes against who you are or what you want. This could result in resentment, a feeling everybody fears to feel because it is the complete opposite of happiness.

Physical Pain

Someone who is depressed is more prone to feeling sick or experience a lack of energy. It causes headaches, cramps, heart palpitations, or trouble breathing in combination with anxiety and digestive problems. Since one's physical health is directly linked to mental and emotional health, the other will suffer the consequences when one is disrupted. When you physically feel unwell, you can address it by reviewing your emotional and mental health first.

These indications can be seen as symptoms of depression that affect many aspects of your life if not addressed. Many people who don't want to acknowledge that they have a problem or accept that they could have this clinical condition may not realize that they have these symptoms. In fact, many people will get so used to living with it. They don't recognize a problem related to it. It's almost as if these symptoms turn into habits—a set of things you do daily without thinking about it at all, like brushing your teeth. You have to do it without considering how it makes you feel. It's similar to how we deal with addiction too. Whether we are aware or not of how harmful smoking or drinking too much alcohol consistently is for us, we do it anyway, every day.

It takes a brave person to recognize that they have depression, admits it, and then addresses it. It's not an easy road to walk. It requires incredible strength, of which the weight could be lifted with adequate support from those around you. To deal with your depression effectively, you have to focus on all wellness variables to ensure you are ready and equipped to take on your depression. It can be done by expressing yourself and sharing your feelings with people you trust. Staying active and setting physical challenges for yourself, combining it with implementing a healthy, nutritious, and balanced diet. When you choose to stand up against depression and deal with it instead of avoiding it, you will gain perspective about the things you do that are harmful to your body. That includes any addictions you may have after considering how it affects you negatively.

There are many other ways to deal with your condition constructively, like staying connected with people in your life and strong building relationships. Asking for help when you need it, and taking a break when necessary because you respect living a balanced life. If you can only do this by living out your dreams and do what you really want to do, it's also suitable to find something you are good at, whether it's a hobby or a career. If looking after yourself means caring about yourself, you should also accept who you are. Instead of judging your shortcomings and flaws, you should embrace them and learn how to practice self-growth. Only then will you pave the way to fulfillment, which is a long journey in itself. Consider this your guide to do just that, and more.

TWO

Talk to Someone

COMMUNICATING WITH PEOPLE CAN APPEAR TO BE THE EASIEST thing in the world until you are depressed. One of the biggest keys to addressing the symptoms of depression is taking a stand and dealing with it. Since you cannot always work through your struggles and feelings by yourself because, let's face it, it rarely helps, it is recommended to talk. To whom, though? Well, anyone who is willing to listen and respect you is perfectly fine. However, talking to someone that knows what they are doing, preferably a psychologist or a doctor is recommended.

Mental health is not the same as one's physical health. There is a bit more to it than just going on a diet or incorporating more exercise into your week to address weight-loss or health concerns. People like to quit after setting a goal with physical health, which can't be the case for mental health. Just like you can't go on a 2-week crash diet and expect to lose weight sustainably and remain healthy at the same time, the same way you can't address depression for a few days or weeks and then stop. You can't half-address mental illness. It's not like a diet that you can adjust or treat according to how you feel. It must be taken seriously. Could you imagine what would happen if you took eating a balanced diet and exercising a few times a week seriously? You would lose all of the weight you've been wishing to lose, improve your health, or finally become more mobile and fit.

Taking this into account, think about what you could achieve if you addressed your mental illness today. Remember, if you leave it, it will remain the same. If you know you have diabetes but don't manage or treat it, your condition will derail, just like any other health condition. The same goes for depression. Dealing with it by yourself isn't an option because without being diagnosed with depression or knowing the severity of your condition, if you indeed have it, you can't treat it. Being medically assessed by a doctor, you can learn more about your symptoms and be advised based on their severity.

It's crucial to know whether you have depression because it has a way of consuming your life. It can control how you feel and obliterate everything that you have ever wanted for yourself. When left untreated, it can become disruptive and affect so many parts of your life. It can even reach a point of becoming so bad that it ruins your life and affects your physical health. One can think of yourself physically sick too, and experience several symptoms as a result. Like it is of utmost importance to look after your mental well-being to support your physical health, it's necessary to stay on top of your emotional health. Like mental health, emotional health plays a vital role in the decisions you make and impacts thoughts, feelings, and the behaviors you display to the world. You can try to hide the fact that you are emotionally unwell or unhappy. Still, it can always be recognized by those who know well, and sometimes, even by people who don't depend on the severity (Xiong G., 2018).

You want to be healthy emotionally because it promotes productivity and makes your life run more effectively. When you are in control of your feelings and emotionality, you will do better at work, school, and anywhere you have to solve problems, perform a task, or deal with people. It plays a role in your relationships' health and longevity, builds character based on the state thereof, and helps you deal with challenges and adversity. Even though it may seem unimportant, it creates balance in all you do in your life, which I don't know about you but makes it pretty important.

Suppose being healthy in all aspects that affect the quality of your life means that you need to see a doctor to address whether you have depression or treat your condition. In that case, it is worth surrendering your pride to make that appointment and show up for it with poise. Strength is within you. All you have to do is wipe the fog from your eyes to see it. Whatever you do, refrain from holding your breath, because it is there.

Seek Help from the Following People

Friends and Family

Anybody who you admire and trust as a supportive person in your life can be easy to open up to—sometimes even more comfortable than a professional. When you open up to the closest people, you will feel relieved that you do not have to continue hiding how you feel. Sharing your feelings with others can even make them seem more bearable because you have people to share them with. This adds a sense of normalcy to them, making it easier for you to address or deal with them.

Specialists

Professionals who specialize in depression, and mental or emotional health, including doctors, supporters, and therapists, can support your journey to better and learn how to live with your condition. For some, depression is a temporary experience. In contrast, it is never-ending for others and is either consistent or occurs every now and again. With this in mind, you need to get help to prevent your condition from becoming permanent or degrading into even more challenging to deal with.

Support Groups

For some people, sharing feelings with a group of strangers seems impossible. Still, it can seem like the best solution to an existing problem for others, especially when you do not want to keep your condition to yourself. Support groups are also fantastic for meeting other people that are experiencing similar struggles as you. Sometimes, it can give you the clarity to talk to people experiencing the same challenges as you. You can expect to hear and share about daily life, struggles, solutions to those struggles in support groups, and gain perspective about your condition as something treatable. In this case, it is not just the clinical condition that makes you feel hopeless or like you are not in control of how you feel.

Helplines

Some people struggle to join a support group because they don't feel like they can share their condition with their friends or family. Others can't even talk about their condition in front of strangers. Luckily, there are hotlines, text lines, and various online support variables with trained volunteers that can help make you feel safer about your conditions. These people play a valuable role in the mental and emotional well-being of many people suffering from depression's lives.

See a Doctor

Depression is an illness that requires a diagnosis from a professional that should provide you with medical attention. Unfortunately, many people are scared to see a doctor as they are afraid to admit something wrong with them. In many cases, this can occur for people who also have a physical medical condition they do not want to address.

As one of the most recognized and disruptive mental

disorders, depression must be treated. People should not feel afraid to visit a doctor. Once you find the courage to seek help, you will discover that it's not so bad after all. Addressing depression and admitting you have it in the first place can be as easy or difficult as you want it to be. What you need to know is that the moment you address it, you can make it better. Perhaps it won't become better instantly. It may even take a little time, effort, and perseverance to get to a point where you feel like it's under control. Taking a step to talk to a professional about it can benefit you in the long haul.

When you feel like your emotional health is negatively impacting your life, it's without a doubt, time to seek support from someone who has the knowledge to address emotional wellness. When you look for a doctor or psychologist, ensure you find one that can provide you with the personalized support you need.

Approaching your emotional wellness, do not think of it as negative to address. Consider it to be something positive. The most your doctor will do for you is prescribing you medication, psychotherapy, or a combination of both to help relieve your symptoms and prevent your condition from disrupting your life. Since there are a few conditions, such as a thyroid disorder that can trigger similar depression symptoms, your doctor may also test you for a few other conditions to ensure you indeed have depression. If you ever feel like you are struggling with feelings that include self-harm thoughts, you should seek medical attention as soon as possible.

Signs you should visit a doctor today:

- Feelings of sadness and hopelessness every day.
- Feelings of guilt, worthlessness, and helplessness.
- Thoughts of self-harm or suicide.
- Loss of interest in hobbies or activities you used to consider entertaining.
- Change in your sleep patterns.

- Feeling tired or lacking the energy to take on your day, regularly.
- Suffering from crying spells.
- Difficulty concentrating, remembering, or making decisions.
- Experiencing aches, pain, and digestive issues that don't improve with treatment.
- Feelings like restlessness, irritation, and annoyance.

THREE

Keep a Journal

IF YOU HAVE EVER KEPT A DIARY, THEN YOU MAY REMEMBER what it felt like to write down your thoughts, feelings, or something that happened on paper. Writing gave you some relief to all you were experiencing at that moment, and just like it did back then, it can now too. Journaling is an excellent medium of self-expression. Instead of keeping everything you think or feel, or perhaps something that happened, to yourself, you get to let it out—about things we otherwise don't dare to talk about. Sure, when you are angry, you can exercise to release energy caused by frustration, and maybe take up boxing to relieve aggression and frustration, but what about everything else?

We all need to unwind our minds, whether it's because something upset you, you don't know how to think clearly based on your feelings, or having too much in your mind that it feels too full to function. Whatever your reason is, journaling can be beneficial to everybody. Although it doesn't seem helpful at first glance, you will realize that there are many benefits to it. Essential to feel much better than you did before you wrote. Think of it as lightening the weight from your mind so that you can think more clearly. It gives you clarity, without a doubt.

Now since you are not a teenager anymore, it can seem unusual to write down how you feel. Or pinpoint events that made you feel negative or fueled your depression. A few years ago, you wouldn't heard of many people who journal. Today, however, it has become popularized. It's considered a form of therapy, a self-care habit. And by writing in your journal every day, it's one of the best and most effective ways to reach your goals. Think of it like this. If your mind is too full or contains unresolved feelings that, let's face it, bothers you, then you can't make clear decisions. You can't set a goal and work your way towards achieving it if there is baggage in your mind. First, you have to deal with it. And, while journaling is not exactly going to solve your problems hands-on, letting everything in your mind run onto paper can clear the way for new thoughts, ideas, and yes, new feelings. Writing about being sad, lonely, or even depressed could potentially open a window for feelings. Such as hope, joy, fulfillment, and give you new energy to take on your day. That's why it is also recommended to journal in the morning or at night.

By writing, you open yourself to gaining a new perspective. The physical actions of writing with your hand and looking at what it is you wrote allow you to review what you wrote. Since it is all out on paper, in front of you, you can think about what you wrote more clearly and consider whether it was really as bad as you thought it was in your mind. Will bad thoughts and feelings magically leave your mind by journaling? No. But, it will provide a safe, quiet space to resonate and think before you react, dwell, or make it worse by overthinking feelings that are usually basic enough to resolve.

Once you have it all in front of you, you can reread it, take it in, and consider solutions to your problems. Possibly implement those solutions or strategize how to implement them, and then move on. Just think what you could accomplish with a fresh slate in your mind. Just imagine what you could achieve.

The Benefits of Unwinding Your Mind

- Provide similar helpful effects as cognitive-behavioral therapy (CBT). It is recommended to reduce symptoms of depression, especially in high-risk cases in children and teenagers.
- Relieves anxiety by calming the mind, provides clarity, and releases depressive feelings and stress. It aids in letting go of negativity, exploring new opportunities. Teaching you more about struggles and successes, enhancing self-awareness, tracking progress when undergoing treatment. Reducing physical symptoms related to health and helping students perform better in tests.
- Allow students to deal with stress by reducing rumination and brooding. It can help students clear their minds of thoughts and feelings right before a test or presentation. It can likewise help someone who has to perform on the spot at work, like speaking in a meeting or giving a speech.
- Improve stress management by allowing a safe space to explore your emotions without being judged or keeping them inside your head. It improves health conditions caused by stress by improving cognitive function, strengthening the immune system, reducing procrastination, and promoting you to take action. Shifting perspective by helping you review your options and consider various outcomes as a result.
- Expressive writing relieves depressive symptoms in

women that struggle with partner violence or emotional abuse. It also reduces negative thoughts that worsen depression.
- Increases awareness as it helps you learn more about yourself. People can be both surprised and shocked by what they pin down on paper. On occasions, it may not seem like there is anything wrong with you until you let your thoughts go. It is not something you should be afraid of, but rather embrace to address them so that you could have better, more positive days. By writing, you will also learn what your worries are, which you can keep to yourself or share with your therapist.
- Reviewing what you write, let's you take control of your depression. It makes whatever you are going through, or feel, seem more bearable and manageable. It diminishes any feelings of hopelessness or worthlessness by helping you gain clarity of reality, which usually is not as bad as you picture in your head.
- Help you track your symptoms and notice patterns that trigger your depression, which gives you clarity on what to treat to figure out how to treat it. Even if you need help treating your triggers, at least you know what they are, and you can begin learning how to reduce or resolve them.

How to Journal the Right Way

To take up journaling, you should:

1. Let your thoughts run free. You can write about anything that comes to your mind and let your thoughts go without worry. When we hold our thoughts to ourselves, we risk stacking up too many things we cannot control. We also start to believe that we can handle our emotions by ourselves,

which nobody really can in truth. Sure, you can work through your feelings, but you have to make an adequate effort accordingly. You can't just think about how you feel and forget about it; that will not resolve anything for you. Instead, it will continue to fill your mind with more things you do not know how to process.

The fantastic thing about writing in a journal is you don't have to tell anyone how you feel until you are ready to. If you want to write everything down, think about it and gain some clarity or derive solutions first, you absolutely can with a pen and paper. When you write, you also shouldn't worry about it being perfect. Just write everything that comes to mind. Let your mind flow into the movement that creates words, and the ink of the ballpoint flows upon meeting paper. Once you are finished, you will be surprised by the things that were pondering in your mind, and you will feel better, too—even lighter if you will.

2.Be ready to write often. Don't just journal once a week or wait until you feel overwhelmed with too many feelings before you pin down all that sits in your mind. It will not work. Journal regularly because whether you realize it or not, all you feel doesn't always show externally. It also does not always trigger your response to feelings or notify you when something is bothering you. You can experience emotions subconsciously too, which contributes to depression. When feelings are left unresolved, that's when fuel gets added to the fire. If you want to be an effective journal writer, you must have a journal, preferably one that looks good and makes you feel better when you look at it. You can even buy a plain black journal and personalize it. However, if you're not one to get creative, pick one of the countless creative journals online. You'll find one that fits you somewhere. Sometimes, even a clean leather does the job just fine, as long as it's soft on the eyes. Get your pens ready, and if you prefer creative journaling versus writing, get a lot of stationary ready.

After you have everything you need, choose a time, and place to commit to writing how you feel. All you need is 20 minutes, which may seem too long to write, but once you start, it will be over before you know it. Plus, as a relaxing activity, it will become enjoyable too. The best recommended time to write is before you start your day in the morning or finish it. You can add a journal session to your morning routine to clear your mind before work. Since journaling is positive, it can set a positive tone for your entire day. Making you feel good and positively affect your job or daily tasks. Opting for an evening journal session, you can write down your thoughts and feelings before bed. Some may consider this a bad idea as it could make them think more. But for clearing your mind, it is quite beneficial for sleeping more soundly as well as waking up without any worries in mind.

3.Don't get bored. Writing the same way every day can become tiresome to some. It may also seem ineffective over time to just write about your day every day. Or perhaps even pin down your feelings and be done with your writing session. There are many other ways you can journal rather than writing the same things over and over again. You can write letters to yourself or other people—without sending it to them, of course. It is a great way to either be appreciative or advising to yourself or potentially resolve any problems or unsaid words between you and other people. This can be people you've argued with, those you feel have misinterpreted you or whom you don't get along with, and somebody who have passed. It can be a way of emitting peace for yourself without having to deal with others. When we are trapped in our emotions, pride, anxiety, or resentment, some cannot handle people face to face. However, there are many other ways to move past the things that are bothering you. As a form of self-love, you can also write positive, inspiring letters to yourself, which can significantly boost your mood.

4.Don't miss the point and dwell. The point of journaling

is not to write about everything negative in your life and then bask in it. The point is to work through all that bothers you wholeheartedly. Dwelling in your sadness or any negative feelings won't get you anywhere. However, writing them down and letting them go or gaining perspective about them will make you feel better. Although journaling is positive, you can fill it with negative thoughts and experiences. Just be sure not to focus on it too much or for too long, as it can turn into a negative experience for you—one that can cause you to dwell in self-pity. If you are afraid of getting caught up in negative journaling, you can always journal your day or feelings. Later, physically throw it away.

5. Journal on the go. Although regular journaling is recommended, you don't have to be so structured that you only write in the designated times. You can carry a small journal in your purse, pocket, or drawer at the office. Wherever you may go, you can take it with you. It is perfect for writing down any thoughts, feelings, or experiences you may have throughout the day. It is especially helpful to write down ideas that enter your mind during the day, instead of letting them go to waste and forgetting about them. Keeping your journal with you can add a little comfort in your life, especially if you know you will be somewhere you'll feel stressed. It can create a sense of consistency in your life to have something with you that relaxes your mind and makes you feel better instantly. It can also help clear your head before taking on new projects, important tasks, or dealing with challenging people, demands, and responsibilities that come your way.

FOUR

Psychotherapy

PSYCHOTHERAPY IS AN ELABORATE WORD FOR "TALK THERAPY." When you consider the simplicity of what it means, it gets a little easier to think of it as a method to fight depression. It is one of the best solutions for dealing with different mental illnesses accompanied by emotional challenges. It can aid in getting rid of, or controlling, symptoms that help people function better. It also increases healing and wellness—two things everybody could use more of in life.

When you get treated for depression, you will be prescribed one of two treatments, or the two combined, which includes medication and talk therapy. Psychotherapy was designed to help people deal with daily life. It can aid in many cases, including helping those who have been impacted by trauma or have difficulty making peace with their past, medical illness, loss of someone close to you, mental disorders, anxiety, and depression. It can also be utilized to treat stress. While psychotherapy is simple to understand, there are a few different types specific to the issue you face. It has been proven an effective treatment method, especially when it gets combined with the right medication.

Therapy sessions can include anything from individual,

group, or couples therapy for any age group ranging from children to adults. Therapy sessions are usually conducted either once or twice a week, depending on your doctor's recommendation. They can be prescribed up to 30 to 50 sessions. With psychotherapy, there's no holding back. It's an engaging activity where both you and your therapist need to be involved in dealing with the problems you struggle with every day. Getting help from a ready and determined professional to help you face everything that troubles you is great because it keeps you accountable. It helps you move through and past your issues effectively. At the end of the day, the goal of this treatment is for it to be effective. That is why your doctor and therapist will decide how many therapy sessions you'll require dealing with everything that derails your mental and emotional well-being.

Similar to journaling, everything you share is kept safe. Therapists are permitted to keep your information and sessions entirely confidential. This can put patients at ease to discuss personal thoughts and feelings they otherwise feel like they can't talk about.

Patients will be happy and relieved to find that most patients who do psychotherapy experience gradual symptom relief that improves their ability to function better in their lives. It works by addressing and improving feelings and behaviors connected to positive brain and body changes. Benefits also include being more energized and reduced physical symptoms of depression and related mental illnesses. As it helps treat depression, it also reduces stress and anxiety. It alters the brain by changing its response to mental illness and has a similar effect on the brain as medication. In this case, patients who don't want to take medication for depression can treat the same psychotherapy symptoms.

When your doctor prescribes therapy for you, you will first receive an assessment from a psychologist. At which point, he or she will specify, apart from how many sessions you need, what type of therapy you need.

Five Primary Therapies

Interpersonal Therapy (IPT)

It is a short-term treatment option that is one of the most common treatment types for depression patients. It helps patients comprehend interpersonal problems that could go unnoticed. These issues are subconscious and may feel troublesome to you in some way; leaving you feeling like you cannot pinpoint them to resolve it. Underlying problems include grief, conflicts in your personal or work relationships and alterations in either your social or professional roles. IPT works well by helping you address your emotions through means of expression. The therapy is also helpful in teaching you how to improve communication. Once you manage these feelings, you can also learn how they affect other issues in your life, which can significantly help treat your depression.

Psychodynamic Therapy

A type of treatment that is centered on the idea of mental and behavioral well-being. The idea is supported by the belief that depression is influenced by childhood experiences, repetitive feelings, or inappropriate thoughts, all of which are unconscious and affect your life somehow. Psychodynamic therapy includes working with a therapist to change existing patterns surrounding bad habits. Improve self-awareness, and implement change to take charge of your life.

Psychoanalysis

This therapy is a more advanced form of psychodynamic therapy. It includes the same process as psychodynamic therapy. Still, it requires patients to have three or more sessions a week to be constructive and helpful. It is implemented in patients diagnosed with severe depression. It is often used to treat people who have thought related to self-harm or suicide.

Dialectical Behavior Therapy

A kind of cognitive-behavioral therapy (CBT) which addresses an emotional imbalance. It is implemented to regulate emotions and your response to them, teaching you how to respond in a better manner to avoid a bad outcome of actions in your responses. It is prescribed to treat anyone with self-harming tendencies, suicidal thoughts, or borderline personality disorder. It is also helpful in treating PTSD and eating disorders, all of which are treated by teaching patients to take responsibility to look after themselves. It aids in changing disruptive behavior and is a hands-on approach by the patient with the support of a therapist to address any problems related to a poor or negative mood. Dialectical behavior therapy can be individual with a therapist or be given in a group.

Supportive Therapy

Therapy focused on guidance and motivation to aid in one's development of unique resources. With this, you are taught to build your self-confidence and self-esteem, strengthen coping mechanisms, reduce stress, reduce anxiety, combat depression triggers, and improve your interactive social functioning. This type of psychotherapy helps patients face reality and deal with their issues by themselves. Especially problems that are caused by depression or other mental conditions that may affect or alter the patient's lives. It creates a positive ground for self-improvement in teaching patients to deal with their struggles.

Other Therapies

There are three other types of treatments you can implement in combination with psychotherapy for it to be even more effective in fighting depression. These include:

Animal-Assisted Therapy

It works by allowing patients to interact with animals. This can be preferably dogs or horses, both of which are animals that can provide a sense of comfort and aid in one's communication skills. Dogs and horses can also help people who have trouble recovering from trauma.

Play Therapy

This therapy, in combination with other psychotherapies for children, is helpful for children to identify emotions and feelings and open up about things that could be bothering them. When a child experiences a traumatic event or stress at a young age, they need to open up about their thoughts and feelings to a professional to help them process underlying depression to avoid it getting worse over time.

Creative Arts Therapy

Art is used to treating many psychological conditions, especially depression. The action of creating something makes one feel as though they are being constructive. It's also enjoyable, which allows people a safe space to express themselves without constraint. This therapy includes painting, dancing, music, drama, poetry, and art journaling.

Replace Negative Thoughts with Positive Constructive Ones

It may seem like fiction, but there is a tried and true way to turn your negative thoughts into positive ones.

Whether it's affirmations, meditation, motivation, and yes, therapy, there are many ways to dismiss your negative thoughts. By rewiring your brain, you can replace them with good and positive, regardless of whether your reality is. What's in your mind is really up to you. Just because you are experiencing a day filled with difficult tasks or things that seem to go wrong does not mean it should result in self-loathing or depreciation. There are ways to take control of your mind.

The truth is, your circumstances will never be perfect. It makes no difference if you are a celebrity or an everyday person struggling to pay his bills. At the end of the day, mindset is everything. If you allow your circumstances to affect your day or your thoughts and feelings, it will. In the same sense, if you allow things to happen to you instead of for you, you will fall short. In essence, it's not what happens to you but what you do with it and how you respond to it accordingly, if you will. The act of assuming command of your life takes self-discipline and the ability to place your well-being first. Those who can't do it will always struggle and be sensitive to the negative obstacles present in their lives.

Since obstacles and challenges will always be there to meet us, we should choose to shake its hand rather than let it get the better of us. If you can find a middle ground of always being in control, no matter what happens or how you are challenged and feel, you will overcome any negativity that steps onto your path.

Of course, even if you have a positive mindset and a neutral set response to anything negative that comes your way, everybody is prone to experience bad days. That's completely normal, and if you feel like having a bad day, so be it. But, never dwell in it. Endure it and then learn from it. Move past it as the strong individual you know you can be. Character development is the key to mastering the voice in your mind that tells you no or keeps you from living up to your potential. With every pitfall, failure, momentary weakness, and negative experience, you build character, but only if you push through it. There is nothing wrong with any of these things as long as you learn from it. That is the key to evolving beyond what you already are and are capable of.

If you can build your character, you can become a force of nature, because if you develop it, you will gain clarity. You will understand why you are responsible for your happiness. You will discover that the key to self-worth lies within you. That it is worthless to seek validation from others or even try to be something other people want you to be, which let's face it, you are probably not. Self-discovery is never too late because we are ever-growing beings. With that, you can change your thought patterns with enough effort and dedication. Yes, mental disorders like depression are serious. Sometimes, taking action against what you have been diagnosed with can change the game for you.

Psychotherapists make use of a technique to treat patients who have depression. This exercise is referred to as turning BLUE thoughts and feelings into true ones. The method is effective in changing your thought patterns, shifting the mindset, and building mental strength.

What is BLUE?

Blaming Myself

When you try to opt for a positive attitude rather than a negative one, you can't blame yourself for things you can't control. In the same breath, you also can't blame yourself for what you lack, don't respect or like about yourself because it isn't productive. What's productive is finding ways to build up your spirits, practice self-love, and be better motivated than you were yesterday. At least that's constructive. When you talk yourself down, however, you are merely doing a disservice to you. It is not helping you or anyone else. Blaming is linked to mental health issues, like excessive unhappiness and depression. Never tell yourself that something is your fault or that you are the root cause of ruin in anything you do. It influences you more than you think, and it's not helpful to you.

Looking For the Bad News

When the average individual considers his or her day, they don't necessarily review the good things that happened to them. No. Instead, they look for the one wrong thing that affected their day. People lean towards anything potentially dramatic. That's why reality shows are so entertaining and popular to watch. When you notice that you or anyone around you explicitly seek bad news, then it's a red flag that you need to put a stop to it immediately. It's not beneficial to anyone to focus on one bad thing that occurred when, in essence, everything else in your day was positive. Highlight this when you experience focusing on the bad things in your day or week.

You'll be astounded how many things there are to be grateful for, especially when you write a positive list and a negative list. When you focus on bad things, and you make a point of focusing on them, you run the risk of creating a habit. A habit you are likely to repeat over and over again until it seems normal to do. Sometimes, people get so caught up in bad habits, like this, that they fail to recognize the potential harm it causes them. That's why it should be addressed, whether you've already built a habit around it, or catch yourself focusing on negative things ever so often.

Unhappy Guessing

The past happened. It's over, and there's nothing you can do to change it, right? Right. The future still has to happen, and there's something you can do to control what happens, right? Right. Since you are living today—not yesterday or tomorrow—you should not focus on what could go wrong on the days you can't control. Just like dwelling in the past doesn't make any sense, thinking about what could go wrong tomorrow doesn't make any sense either.

Instead of worrying yourself to death, embrace the present, face your challenges when they occur and don't do something because of what you think could go wrong. This way of thinking constricts you. It holds you back, which is the very last thing you want if the point of your life is reaching a balanced point of fulfillment like it is for us all. Considering that thinking about everything that could go wrong will affect your mood negatively, you may also want to avoid it if you are trying to opt for a positive approach to life.

Exaggerated Negative

When something doesn't go your way, the last thing you should do is dwell in it or makes it out to be worse than it is. So you didn't pass your interview, or you didn't score as high as you wanted to on a test. Perhaps you even froze when you were delivering a presentation or failed to impress someone in a social setting. Rather than beating yourself up about it or staying in a negative headspace, thinking about it and looking back to it as often as you can, don't. Move on from it immediately. If you need a moment, feel free to take a second to consider what happened, but find a bright side to it. You are not going to be perfect in everything you do, especially not if you are human. So, bite the dust, and move on, my friend. The more negatively you approach the things you do wrong, the more negative it will be. The fate of your feelings is in your hands. Truly.

The goal of adopting the BLUE method is replacing bad or negative thoughts with improved ones to achieve a better outcome and build positive habits that promote stable feelings. Instead of opting for a negative approach to all you do, you can choose a positive one. This helps anyone who needs to adopt a positive approach to the way they think. Once this is done, you will be more inclined to opt for positive feelings over negative ones because you won't create negative situations for yourself. You will learn to opt for positivity, and with time, it will transcend into a natural act of self-worth—something we all need.

Find Coping Strategies

Different psychotherapy formats are designed to treat either individual cases or multiple people at once. As discussed, therapy can be delivered in one of six primary treatments, in conjunction with one or more psychotherapy formats.

These formats include:
Individual Therapy

This therapy type is recommended one-on-one with a professional psychologist. The patient requires full attention to resolve their depression. Any causes, influencing factors, or implications of depression must be addressed during a session with your therapist. This is a solution that should be derived between the two of you. It helps patients receive one-on-one therapy sessions as it allows patients to work through any issues they may have. Frequently, people hide their thoughts, opinions, and feelings. They fear to confide in their family, friends, and those they spend their time with because they fear judgment or disrupting their privacy. In this case, the only option for them is to turn towards a therapist that could give them a safe area to let go and speak their truth. This usually helps them overcome the worst of their depression.

In individual therapy, once you reach a certain point, therapists may suggest you share your journey with depression with someone or multiple people closest to you to gain adequate support, but this, of course, is voluntary. When a patient requests individual therapy, they usually don't want to involve their family or friends into their struggle with depression. In this case, individual therapy is recommended to reach a point of development and recovery past depression before building up the courage to inform the people they need to resolve underlying issues.

Group Therapy

An approach recommended for anywhere between three to fifteen people allows everyone to add their opinion and talk about their personal feelings within a group. This type of therapy is perfect for families or co-workers who have experienced a traumatic event together or have difficulty getting along with one another. It allows therapists to interact with participants as a group, often combined with individual therapy to address depression. This type of therapy is also less expensive than individual therapy.

Family Therapy

Like group therapy, family therapy is excellent for resolving challenges and dynamics that disrupt peace in families. Family therapy is especially helpful for couples who have children that suffer from depression and is recommended for families that are either processing a death in the family or undergoing a divorce. It can also be beneficial when a significant event occurs in the family, or if parents feel like their children require attention to deal with emotional and mental health conditions.

Couples Therapy

A therapy that only involves two people. It is suited for married couples or anyone in a committed relationship that is experiencing troubles. It is suitable for improving functioning in a relationship, which can help resolve many issues before marriage and address current marriage problems. Given the current divorce rate in the U.S., which is up to 60% for couples that get married within the age of 20 and 25, and about 45% for couples who marry at 25-years old and above, one would say couples therapy is needed to potentially safeguard every marriage in America (20 Divorce Facts for 2020, n.d).

Learn Problem-Solving Techniques

The goal of psychotherapy is to identify the issues you face in your life, whether internal or exterior contributing factors. By talking to a professional, you establish these things, which, once established, can then be addressed to be resolved. People who suffer from depression are usually caught up in their feelings and spend most of their time fixating on the way things are in their minds. Without saying aloud that they accept their feelings, they surrender to them subconsciously and don't realize the harm they inflict upon themselves. It is a big problem, as it is one of the leading factors contributing to depression, anxiety, and other emotional or mental health concerns.

While the general notion is to fixate on the things we believe we can't change, it makes more sense to concentrate on the things you can change or finding a solution to the things you think you can't change. It can be done successfully by learning how to solve problems and be done adequately with the help of an action plan designed to help you solve any issues you may have. Whether they are as bad as you imagine or not. Problem-solving things that bother you mean to actively solve your problems in your personal and professional life.

These six steps can be implemented to solve problems successfully.

Identify the Problems That Affect Your Life

Countless issues successfully hinder people every day. Some people feel like they can't catch a break. If there is something even remotely troublesome seen in their mind, be it a bad thought or experience, it affects them. Whereas, others are much less affected and often unphased by things that occur, whether it is in your mind as a thought or feeling, or real experience. Now, those who react or have an emotional response to everything that could potentially upset them require some time to distinguish a line to indicate what is acceptable to be affected over and what is not. When you are overly sensitive, this can be difficult to do. It's almost like you need to alter yourself, but luckily, not for those around you. Instead, it's for yourself because being too sensitive can create many problems in your life. It could initiate unnecessary ideas and feelings and contribute to issues that you could have possibly created yourself.

Have you ever wondered how some people are not troubled by negativity or a bad event? It's because they have a line drawn that they won't overstep unless it's necessary. Of course, you can't tell someone to be less sensitive. It's a difficult process that needs to be addressed all by yourself. Knowing that it can be managed, that change starts within, and that you can choose to be a problem-solver, instead of a creator, is the first step in the right direction. Suppose you can identify the problems that affect your life. In that case, you can create two categories and contemplate which are actually worth being bothered about, and which aren't. The fewer battles you fight with yourself or anyone else, and the less affected you are by random things happening around you, the more power you will have to take control of your feelings, triggers, and ultimately, your life.

Once you address the problem(s), you can start initiating a solution(s). This could be you, the presence of certain types of people in your life, your job, personal fulfillment, or a lack thereof, to name a few.

Research Before Overthinking or Misinterpreting

If you can perceive a clear view of the problems you need to solve to move past your depression or related mental issues, you need to get your facts straight about the nature of your struggles and discover the causes. It can be done by looking into similar issues people had to resolve or consult a therapist to help guide you to move past them. Once you know what you need to address, you can do so with ease, knowing that there is no need to be ashamed. Even if you need to work on yourself and implement a little self-discovery or development, take charge of your life. Finding what will resolve your problems is heroic.

You should be proud of addressing your problems because, with depression, it can be challenging for patients to even start. Many people also don't want to accept that they play a significant role in their problems or think they have. It is usually the case for anyone who spends too much time thinking. Most of the time, unless you have experienced patterns or recurring difficulty and experiences in your life, have undergone traumatic events or instances, or have structured your life in the wrong way, depression is fueled internally. Recognizing that whatever you give your mental energy to is what will be is an excellent reminder to not stumble into the trap of needless things ruling your life. What you need to realize is that you are in control.

Seek Solutions and Don't Give Up

Just like you have made every decision that has led you to this point, you can create new choices to change things. You can take control of your life, and no one can do it but you. You should realize that. Once you do, you can take back control of your life. When you can see that you can take control, you will resist negative things present in your life. Especially people or doing things that goes against your inner being. Apart from discovering your problems, you can find the solutions to them by finding out what you need. You have to be selfless first to be a positive source in other people's lives and thrive in your own life. Without truly looking after yourself and working on self-fulfillment, you could question your self-worth. If you do that, you won't have the power to derive solutions to combat inner conflicts. That is mainly because you won't have a purpose and will continue seeking meaning without knowing that it lies within yourself. When you are in control of your emotional and mental wellbeing, things start to get good, and you are sentenced with the idea that you want to live your best life. So, in essence, finding solutions becomes the only option for you.

Decide, Implement Action, and Become Disciplined

With a curated list of solutions and a solution-only mindset, you can find the best answers to the problems you have that contribute to your depression. When you put yourself first and value your life, happiness, the things you want and care about, it's all crystal clear. Now that you have the best solutions, you can put it to the test and take action. If it doesn't work or go the way you intended entirely, you can always finetune it as much as necessary to help solve your problems. Just because you have solutions and work hard to implement them, don't be rash, and think that they will instantly change your life.

Happiness starts within. You can't wait to be happy, which is why addressing internal issues are crucial. When you manage to resolve yourself, the rest will be easy to do, even if you have to let go of some people, find a new career or job, and do what is best for you. Before you make any decisions you could resent going forward, be sure to take your time and don't rush anything. Internal happiness is like a tunnel you have to shovel with a teaspoon.

Wait For the Results Before Reacting

When you are on your journey, you can decide whether there is more to be done. You can see where you need to work on yourself or other aspects of your life. As you do this, over time, the picture will become more apparent. You can give yourself time to observe everything you are implementing before following up or deciding when you have reached a good point to take things slower. You don't have to go full speed all the time. You will notice when things start to pivot in your life. When it does, be happy that you managed to address your problems, whether it was with the help of a therapist, your family, friends, support groups, or yourself.

To become solutions-oriented, you need to be creative to solve your problems. You will have to brainstorm solutions to your problems. If you have depression, you have probably been stuck in your mind for a while. Therefore, this means that you will need to think outside the box to find new approaches to solve the problems you have been sitting with for a long time. Imagine staring into a cement wall. You can walk a mile to the right to get around it and discover something new. However, instead of doing this, you only walk a few steps and decide that you are stuck, so that's all you will be.

Combining creativity with logical thinking can help you diagnose potential causes of the problems you face to conclude the best solutions for you. With analytical skills and systematic processes, you can think clearly and make new decisions about moving forward. Even if you feel you lack something to work through your feelings, you don't. You simply have to work on finding solutions to deal with the things that seem impossible to you. If you are dealing with interpersonal conflict, for instance, you can deal with it effectively by developing your emotional intelligence. Focusing on your decision-making skills will also help you plan to make decisions and see them through too. When you decide to do something, you shouldn't be hesitant about it. You should force yourself to do it. Although it may be a challenge, getting comfortable with getting uncomfortable can be a great initiative to push self-growth.

To improve problem-solving skills, you should:

- Be committed to finding a solution.
- Define the problem or multiple problems.
- Choose a constructive process.
- Become an active listener.

FIVE

Set Goals

IF YOU WISH TO LIVE A BETTER LIFE, SETTING GOALS IS THE answer for you. Without goals, it seems impossible to remain accountable in anything you do, including overcoming depression. If you want to overcome this challenge, you must have an action plan broken down with smaller benchmarks. Overcoming depression is not easy. It's big and requires action. Suppose you are serious about improving your life. In that case, you will have to fully commit yourself to creating goals and then achieving them sustainably.

Anybody suffering from depression is recommended to receive counseling or therapy. If you have already reached this step, you know that a lack of planning won't get you anywhere. Thus, your plan must be detailed and concise. It must include micro-goals that are achievable and don't deliver temporary results, but long-term results. When you set goals, you will be inspired to achieve them, but if they take too long to achieve, or the micro-rewards don't seem too great, you may lose your motivation to keep going. In this case, you should review your list of goals. Consider setting goals for things you actually want to achieve—only things that will be fulfilling and make a positive difference in your life.

Without losing sight in therapy, which at first can seem scary to you, consider setting the following goals to improve your experience to achieve a desirable outcome:

- Change your behavior, and how changing it will benefit your mood and help you address your depression with a solution-oriented approach that starts with you.
- Improve your ability to create and maintain healthy relationships.
- Enhance the effectiveness and your ability to cope with everyday challenges.
- Choose a decision-making approach to change your life.
- Focus on self-development.

You can use these goals to stay motivated and focused on making a positive change in your life. If the point of therapy or self-development is to work through your depression. It is to achieve a positive change in your life, following through and doing what you need to do to get ahead should be a priority. Once you can accomplish this, you can start navigating your life to achieve personal and professional goals. At this point, who knows, you may be inspired to reach your goals the first time around.

When you start counseling, be realistic about what you want to achieve. Don't limit yourself in thinking you can't achieve something, be clear about your expectations, and motivations to make impactful changes.

Use these steps to get started:

1. Identify goals.
2. Decide where to start.
3. Identify what is required to smash goals.
4. Take one step at a time for sustainable results.

So often, it can feel like your goals are empty shells without a grain of sand inside. But what you don't know—usually for those who have been unsuccessful in achieving goals—is that you are surrounded by sand. So, you have to move. You have to:

G - Goal
R - Reality
O - Options
W - Way Forward

Solutions are everywhere around you. Don't stay inside your head. Keep the GROW acronym in mind when you feel like giving up again.

Consider A GROW Model Before Quitting
1. Goal

- Why did you set this goal, and what did you want to achieve from it?
- How significant is it to you to achieve it?
- Are your goals overconfident or unrealistic without a plan?
- What will indicate that you are achieving your goal?
- How will you feel once you have achieved your goal?
- Can you adjust the process to achieve your goal more efficiently, and is there something you can do to achieve it more quickly?
- How will achieving it impact your life, and how will it make you feel?
- Are there any negatives to achieving this goal, and will it keep you from putting in the work to achieve your goal?

2. Reality

- Are you realistic about your goals?
- How is the progress on your goals? Are you where you thought you'd be, or did you achieve what you initially thought you would achieve by this point in time? Ask yourself regularly.
- Have you implemented action to support your micro-goals to achieve your macro goal(s)?
- What results have you achieved to this point, and are you pleased with your progress?
- Are you struggling to achieve micro-goals, and if yes, how can you adjust it to achieve a more realistic result?

3. Options

- Have you explored a range of options to achieve your goal(s)?
- Can you think of other ways to move forward?
- What have you learned from the process thus far?
- Are there pros and cons for each of these options

4. Way Forward

- When you achieve your goal, what will you do?
- What obstacles could you potentially face?
- Rate your success on a scale of 1 to 10 with regards to your achievements. Did you do the best you could? Are you proud of how you performed?
- Is it possible for you to plan ahead to develop more constructive strategies in the planning stage before attempting to achieve your goal(s)?
- Which three micro-steps can you take to bring yourself closer to reaching a micro goal in 24 hours?

Caring about yourself is the best way to get started on your journey to achieve a goal. If you do not care about yourself, you will be likely to quit your goals. When someone is depressed, you will discover that they quite often don't care about or have respect for themselves. Because, thinking of someone who does care and respect themselves, you could imagine that such a person would want to feel good, get better, be happier, and improve their entire life.

SIX

Identify Issues That Contribute to Depression

As one of the primary mental and emotionally constraining disorders that exist, depression still doesn't get talked about enough. Sometimes, it gets briefly discussed in society. Still, there is hardly ever elaborated information made available to society about it unless you research it yourself. Many people struggle with identifying depression, which can be because they are either uninformed, in denial, or scared to admit that they are more than just sad. Although it can be scary, identifying the cause thereof can help you derive a solution.

What Causes Depression?

Life Events

When something bothers you, especially for a long time, it can have an emotional effect on you, recognized and not. When you suppress feelings, thoughts, or ideas, it's a clear indication that something is not right. Life events can affect us in more ways we could ever imagine. They have a way of affecting us, mainly if it happens during our childhood years. Anything remotely traumatic or shocking that occurs will remain in your mind for years and sometimes hold on your entire life. It can include unemployment, abusive or disruptive relationships, isolation, loneliness, work stress, family pressure, and many other life stresses. Apart from childhood experiences, you can also be negatively affected by a combination of events that trigger depression, which can also be fueled by personal factors.

Personal Factors

Family history, personality, serious medical illnesses, and addiction are primary individual factors that can cause depression.

Family History

This can result in increased genetic risk for depression, so it's necessary to know your family history. If it is genetic, you can start to treat and learn how to deal with it at a young age.

Personality

This represents a vital role in the development of depression. It can add to the presence of the symptoms thereof. For example, if you are very sensitive, you are more likely to feel negative feelings. Things that happen will affect you more deeply than anyone who is not as sensitive. It is just one example. The more your personality is adjusted to being in control, the more likely you will resist anxiety, depression, or emotional disruptions. Personality can make people more at risk of being depressed, possess low self-esteem, and increase sensitivity to personal criticism and negativity.

Medical Illnesses

When you already have a mental or emotional disorder, you will be more prone to manage the way you feel. Depression is often combined with other mental disorders. Suppose you do suffer from a mental disorder. In that case, depression is likely to follow if you don't have your emotional and mental health under control.

Addictions

Alcohol and drug abuse can make you more prone to

develop depressive tendencies. Primarily because they are generally used to combatting their feelings and, ideally use as a coping mechanism.

Changes in the Brain

The brain is the most complex organ in the body. Still, today, there is a lot we don't understand about it, including the chemical reactions that occur in it. Depression is usually mistaken for only being caused by a chemical imbalance in the brain. Whether you have an imbalance or not, many other factors contribute to depression. There is genetic vulnerability, life stressors, substances like medications, drugs, alcohol, and medical conditions related to your mood regulation.

To address chemical imbalances in your brain, modern antidepressants that affect your chemical transmitters like noradrenaline and serotonin, are usually prescribed—this type of medication aids in transferring messages between brain cells. With the help of psychological treatment, you can also improve and regulate your mood effectively. Therapy can also stimulate the growth of brand-new nerve cells and brain circuits that regulate your mood. This is recommended by general practitioners as the ideal solution to recover from severe depression. It is usually their number one choice of treatment when presented with a case of depression.

Keeping these causes of depression in mind, you should take note that every person is different. Just because someone you know has depression due to one reason does not mean it is the same for you. Suppose you are concerned about having depression, whether mild or severe. In that case, you should consult your doctor and not be afraid of the treatment options they present you with.

SEVEN

Practice Mindfulness

THOUGHTS HAVE A WAY OF TURNING INTO FEELINGS, AND pondering has a way of turning into something far beyond what we want to accept. It can be real or false, but it's almost always real to us when caught up in it, regardless of the truth.

Mindfulness can be used to treat depression effectively. It is one of the many things you can implement to combat and gain control over everything that impacts your life.

Mindfulness-Based Cognitive Therapy (MBCT) is a treatment option designed to recognize and control negative thoughts. It could do more than just prevent you from experiencing a brief moment of feeling sad, lonely, or anything else that depression ultimately makes you feel. MBCT is an eight-week structural program that is focused on mindfulness with the help of cognitive-behavioral therapy. It is a powerful program used to treat mild and severe cases of depression. Suppose you think about it unless passed onto you through genetics or diagnosed with a mental disorder accompanied by depression. In that case, it's the only thing standing between your success in moving past depression and negative feelings is your mind itself. The one thing you can control, but one thing many people think they can't control. That's it. It is as simple as that.

What does it mean to be mindful?

It means being aware of your emotions, thoughts, and how you feel mentally and physically. It is a type of meditation with the presence of self-acceptance. It creates self-awareness about your thoughts and emotions without any judgment.

Cognitive therapy is the general option for treating depression. It teaches patients how to notice negativity and redirect it into positivity—whether it's self-talk, a manner of thinking, or feeling. With mindfulness, one can work on fixing thoughts and feelings that are affected by negativity.

When we are negative or anxious, we get sucked into our emotions, when things start to go wrong. By combining mindfulness with cognitive therapy, like implementing meditation, you can start feeling more positive about yourself. You can diminish anxiety or emotional reactions by understanding why you feel the way you do and learning how to resolve them or combat them. The combination of mindfulness and cognitive therapy makes the MBCT technique work. It helps you develop a habit to prevent thoughts of taking control.

You should always be in control, and that is the purposeful key to fighting depression. Suppose you can build a habit that keeps you grounded. Aware of what you are doing when you are doing it and how it will impact you, the people around you, and the quality of your life. In that case, you will see more reason into what it is you are doing, thinking, and even feeling. You can condition yourself to become resistant against anything that keeps you from being the best version of yourself. Or may cause you to neglect a positive, happy, and content version of yourself. If the point is to prevent your thoughts from controlling you, you have to take time to take control of your thoughts. If you don't give them permission to rule or hold on your life and the outcome of your day, they won't.

When in doubt, how to take control, try this technique for mindful meditation:

1.Sit up straight and maintain a good posture while sitting on a chair. Double-check your spine is supported from top to bottom and place your feet next to each other on the floor, facing the front.

2.Close both eyes and keep them closed. Then, use your mind to focus on your breath while it flows in and out. It is mindful breathing with intention. Notice your sensations but don't judge them. Be kind to them, and don't try to breathe slower or faster. Keep it rhythmic and calm.

3.After breathing intentionally for a while—a few minutes—allow your mind to wander and shift your attention back to breathing. Realize that you have allowed your mind to wander with your permission and bring it back to your breathing. This idea is critical.

4.Once completed, your mind will be calm. This can be repeated every day for at least 20 to 30 minutes to practice mindfulness successfully.

This technique will teach you how to practice mindfulness until it becomes a natural choice in your day in everything you do. Including how you respond to thoughts, feelings, people, and experiences.

EIGHT

Connect the Body and Mind

THERE ARE VARIOUS REASONS YOU SHOULD STRIVE TO DO THE best you can to connect to your body and mind. After all, it is what keeps you well and secures your health. The body receives signals from your brain and vice versa. With your mind collecting signals from your body to ensure it performs harmonically, your body also receives messages to function adequately. Without the one performing optimally, the other cannot operate or know what to do. This is why paying attention to both, and establishing a connection to create awareness between the two, is of utmost importance.

If you want to reach good health in all aspects of your life, including your emotional health in this case—thoughts, behaviors, and feelings—you must find a balance in your life. It can only be done when you implement healthy and constructive ways to deal with stress, anxiety, and establish that it is normal when presented with problems. It forms an essential part of life, which you can choose to be in control of. If you are blessed with physical health, you owe it to yourself to sustain it without any health concerns. The same goes for your mental and emotional health. People who live with illnesses, disabilities, or are challenged physically seemingly have more perspective. They don't think to themselves, "I can't do this, and therefore I will be negative and self-deprecating for the rest of my life."

No. Most people that are constrained physically are some of the most appreciative people you will ever meet. They are generally very positive. Even though this is not consistently the case, it is for many people. Imagining this, if you are entirely in control of your physical health, you have a lot to be grateful for and can't complain about. It is necessary to maintain a positive perspective and focus on what you have and not on what you don't. Optimal health starts with being content with what you have. Putting in the work to address what you possibly lack, like what you perceive as the inability to control your emotions and mental health.

By teaching yourself how to deal with various factors that negatively affect you, you can look past the restrictions you have placed in your mind and overcome them. Learning how to manage planned and unplanned emotions, like sadness, stress, anxiety, and loneliness, you stand a better chance of dealing with unwanted changes. These can include anything from losing a job, being demoted or promoted, coping with grief, getting married, or divorced. As well as experiencing conflict with people closest to you, suffering from an illness, getting into an accident, having a baby, moving homes, and enduring money problems. Since your body responds to how you feel, think, and act, learning how to react positively to all these occurrences is significant to maintain a healthy mind-body connection. The moment you feel a terrible feeling related to stress, anxiety, or negativity, you should know that something isn't right. Whether you accept it or not, it does impact your health. It can increase your blood pressure, heart rate, weaken your immune system, and cause a stomach ulcer with excessive stress and worry.

If you wish to be in command of your health, one of the things that need to be addressed, apart from the food you eat or the exercise you do, is taking control of how you respond to life. Once you recognize your emotions, you should try to understand the reasons why you are experiencing them. By working through the causes of any negative feeling or what influences your health, you can start the journey to obtain improved wellbeing.

Start To Recognize Your Emotions

Express Emotions Appropriately

A lack of self-expression is something many people suffer from. While it may seem like you don't want to burden anyone with your feelings and troubles, there are ways to express yourself healthily without feeling like you are weak. You are emotionally strong when you build up the courage to, instead of hiding your feelings, say what you feel. By keeping your feelings inside, all you are doing is disrupting your inner peace. Suppose you don't tell anyone how you feel. In that case, nobody will know what your emotions are or what is going on in your life, and when you become reserved, that's when you start to distance yourself from others. You are not only bottled up with emotions that you can't express, but you are disconnected from the world. It will make your reality seem even worse as you may feel misunderstood and alone in the things you have to deal with.

Instead of trying to be strong all the time, whether you are a man or a woman, realize that your family and friends are there to help you. Or, they are supposed to be, to a certain extent. If you can't rely on your family or friends, then who can you rely on? They are not there to only bask in the good you have to offer. Their role also encompasses comfort, support, and the passing of wisdom to aid in your growth journey. If you feel like you can't get empathy or support from those around you, consult a doctor, religious advisor, or counselor. Whatever it is you are feeling, you do not have to go through it alone.

Live a Balanced and Synergic Lifestyle

Gratitude plays a massive role in stabilizing the relationship you have with life itself. When you are grateful for what you have instead of focusing on what you don't have, you understand what is important. When you review your life over time, you will come to realize what makes sense versus what does not. With this, you will discover that wealth, materialism, and status are all meaningless without love, peace, trust, and joy in your life. Unfortunately, what you own or what your title is, does not aid in achieving any of these things. Love, peace, and trust start with you. Even joy is initiated by you within you. You are the answer to everything you truly need. What follows is a by-product thereof. For instance, if you are a workaholic and gain a lot of money, but you do not have time to build a family, do you think you will be happy sustainably going forward? The thought about money is that it doesn't keep you company when you're old. Do not mistake excitement for happiness because excitement is temporary. Real happiness is within, and can only be achieved with self-acceptance and having elements in your life in check.

Equally, when you encounter difficulties or challenges in your life, try to not obsess over them as this will only fuel negativity in your life. Achieve balance by prioritizing the essential things, and choose positivity whenever you can. Even if a situation seems dire, seek the good in it, even if it's just to learn from what you have experienced. The key to finding balance is to deal with negative feelings by focusing everything positive in your life. You will find it valuable to keep a journal about every positive moment in your day. This you can reflect on at the end of your day or the start of the next, to prevent focusing on the negatives. Whatever is making you feel overwhelmed or stressed, you should let go of it. If you have a moment to think clearly about your worries, nothing will present itself as bad as it seems.

Implement Resilience

Resilience is the ability to overcome swiftly from difficulties. It is the measure of your mental toughness. People who are prisoners to depression or anxiety may lack mental toughness. However, everything can be taught if you are willing to learn. If you are resilient, you have a better chance of coping with the stress life presents you with, and as a result, resist negative thoughts and feelings that contribute to depression and anxiety. Resilience can be learned and powered with strategies. Such as receiving adequate social support, maintaining a positive perspective about who you are and how you view yourself, accept change, and consider all things with a clear perspective. Professional therapists can support you in reaching this goal by implementing these strategies sustainably with cognitive behavioral therapy.

Become Calmer

If you are stressed out, like many of us are ever so often, your mind and body are not at peace. Stress and the effects of anxiety cause far more issues in our bodies than we would like to notice. We can often be very resistant to them, and with this, we fail to recognize that we don't have control of our peace. When your body-mind connection works together in harmony, both are relaxed. Stress is the leading cause of disruption in the body, causing the mind to become uneasy. The body becomes ill or symptomatic. It's crucial to integrate relaxing techniques into your life because life can become one big stress ball. Think of it as a pile of candy floss, with grains of rice stuck in it, and all you have to pick the rice out are chopsticks. You're never going to get the rice out of the candy floss, are you? You cannot let stress get the better of you. Suppose you are not practicing how to be calm. In that case, your mind and body are likely disrupted and succumb to stress automatically by now.

Suppose you want to find a balance between your mind and body to support each other in all you do or endure. In that case, you can implement relaxation practices. These include Tai Chi, yoga, meditation, listening to music, and imagery tracks. Stretching, accompanied by adequate breathing, is also a great way to calm your body. By focusing on your breathing, you can learn to transcend proper breathing into your everyday life. With this, you will be able to breathe more mindfully in all you do, which will prevent you from reacting to stress and anxiety and deal with it constructively instead.

Practice Self-Care

Taking care of yourself is obvious. We all recognize that we should brush our teeth, bathe, keep groomed, eat a healthy diet, exercise regularly, and get enough sleep, right? Apart from that, though, there is more to self-care than just the basics. You must maintain emotional wellbeing, take care of yourself by looking after your body, and allow yourself time to relax. You also have to avoid bad habits like overeating, dehydration, sleeping too little, abuse alcohol, drugs, or cigarettes. With that, it's necessary to stay on top of your health. Visit your doctor on schedule for your annual checkups, and address anything that may be physically, mentally, or emotionally wrong. Since it is your body and you only have one, you have full ownership of it, and thus, you are the only one who can care for it. So, you should, and do so with respect and loyalty. A healthy and cared-for body will take you through life with ease and won't let you down before your time runs out.

Acupuncture

As one of the oldest, yet modern relaxation techniques today, you have probably heard of acupuncture before. It is recognized as a practice where small needles get placed onto your body to relieve strain.

Yes, there is not too much else to it, except for its benefits, which not many people know. Acupuncture dates back 2,500 years ago in China, where it originated as a significant part of Traditional Chinese Medicine (TCM). Practitioners use this relaxation technique to stimulate specific areas of the body, treat various conditions, and target pressure points that are most prone to the build-up of stress. Although acupuncture hasn't always been so popular today, it has come a long way. One of China's most effective treatments has been adopted globally as a naturopathic medical practice to relieve osteoarthritis and menstrual pain. Since it relieves tension, it is recommended to boost one's mood and balance the body. With a sound body, the Chinese believe that you have a better feeling of being in control of your body and mind.

Working its way into the Western world of medicine, it is now considered one of the most effective stress-relieving practices in the U.S. to relieve depression and anxiety.

According to Traditional Chinese Medicine, acupuncture works by balancing the flow of energy throughout your body. It is referred to as "qi," which moves through your body on meridians—energy channels. When the meridians become blocked, it results in illness that causes physical symptoms like aches and pains in the body or symptoms that suggest you are emotionally strained, like stress and anxiety. Acupuncture removes blockages and aids in restoring natural and harmonious energy levels, bringing balance to your mind, body, and organs. It allows everything to work in sync with one another.

Although there hasn't been much research done about its effectiveness in treating depression, calming your mind-body connection, and releasing tension from your whole body is one of the most useful treatment options. Acupuncture is a form of self-care. So, even if you don't feel depressed or anxious, going for a session once or twice a month can benefit you in many ways. Treat stress in your body before it becomes worse. Since most people have difficulty relaxing today—generally, the cause of stress, depression, and anxiety—acupuncture is a solution to keeping your wellness in check.

Although it is not a science-based treatment, Western medicine suggests that it releases endorphins in your body. The body's natural painkillers to boost body and brain functioning that treats or relieves painful symptoms.

Massage

One of the most popular stress-relieving treatments that exist today is massage therapy. You can get a massage at a spa or done by a professional therapist specializing in treating aches and pains in the body. Massage therapy manages the muscles and soft tissue in your body to promote functioning and relaxation. Apart from that, it is also used to unwind and often gets recommended as a treatment option to reduce stress levels and practice self-care.

Just like acupuncture, massage therapy originated from China but was discovered before it, 3,000 years ago. Ancient practitioners of massage therapy found that it eased feelings associated with depression or a generally negative mood. It provided people with clarity to take on the day with a motivated approach. The Chinese also believed that touch combined with pressure released hormones that create an emotional connection. Today, people can resonate with the beliefs surrounding massage therapy's effectiveness. Most people go for a massage to calm their minds, relieve aches and pains, and improve their moods, mainly if they are overstressed.

It helps relieve depression by addressing muscles and connective tissues in the body when it becomes stiff or rigid. When muscles and connective tissues are bruised or overused, it causes pain and limits movement. Something massage therapy can address by relieving tension and increasing blood flow to the body's affected areas. When you opt for a massage therapy as a treatment option, note that it is not a treatment option for depression. But one that can treat symptoms, therefore, as part of a treatment plan. The therapy can alleviate joint pain, back pain, sluggishness, muscle aches, relieve fatigue, and sleep issues. Therapy involves various types of massages, including:

Swedish Massage

The application of smooth, circular, kneading actions to affected muscles.

Deep Tissue Massage

A method used to treat muscles that are tight as a result of stress. This massage is focused on deep muscles that are located the closest to your connective tissues and bones.

Chair Massage

A process that specifies you to sit on a treatment chair and lean forward to place your head into a headrest for support. This type of massage is short and can introduce the body to more intense massages that could be a little painful at first.

Reflexology

A method that involves applying pressure to your feet triggers correspondence with systems and organs in the body, providing relief to areas in your body that are otherwise difficult to treat.

Shiatsu

A technique that requires a therapist to apply pressure to specific body points, similar to acupuncture, to release tension. This treatment option causes stiffness and headaches at first and should be eased into smaller, less intense sessions.

Aromatherapy

A massage method is used in combination with scented oils to reduce stress and simultaneously boost energy.

Hot Stone Massage

Massage therapy involves the placement of hot stones onto your body to relax your muscles individually. The pressure is applied to the stones to relieve deep muscle tension.

Meditation

This form of natural treatment for depression and anxiety is a given. Depression is a big problem many people, both young and old, face today. It affects more people than we realize and increases the risk of suffering from heart disease and other illnesses. Combined with depression, people are also more prone to dying from illnesses instead of working to fight it. It affects our daily lives, and if not ours, people around us for sure. It can make people feel socially isolated and misunderstood. Affect cognitive functioning, and alter one's ability to remember. Usually, because the mind is too focused on everything that is going wrong. It impairs the brain's ability to recall experiences and events due to the stress associated with any unsettling feeling. People older than 65 who suffer from depression are likely to have an episodic memory that impairs their memory. As treatment options, prescribed therapy, and medication are generalized as primary, meditation can help you on your journey to fighting depression for a more natural approach. That is because the meditative practice can help you change how your brain responds to stress and negativity.

Meditation trains your brain to develop a sustained focus that can alter thoughts and feelings' automatic choice. If you are used to opting for negative or unhappy thoughts and feelings, you can use meditation to shift your perspective. It provides you with a positive, energized, and constructive approach to the things you deal with or experience. By altering your focus and maintaining it, you will get into the habit of naturally changing your thoughts and feelings. You will only choose positivity and wellness instead of resorting to sadness, loneliness, experiencing a lack of self-worth, and feelings associated with feeling lost, angry, unhappy, misunderstood, and unfulfilled.

Meditation also takes on brain regions directly linked to depression. When you are depressed, your medial prefrontal cortex (mPFC), also recognized as the "me-center," becomes hyperactive and out of control. It causes you to worry and misinterpret information about yourself, especially when you get stressed out. The amygdala has a similar function. It is recognized as the "fear center" of your brain and gets placed under strain, and when it does, it doesn't know how to respond. It is responsible for your fight-or-flight response, and when under pressure, you can just imagine what your brain chooses. By triggering the adrenal glands, it releases the stress hormone, cortisol, which is your direct response to potential danger and fear.

The two brain regions, the mPFC and the amygdala, work with one another to cause depression. If these two regions can be controlled and taught to react better to feelings of stress, anxiety, and fear—all of which causes a spike in cortisol levels that places strain on the mind, then you can become in control of your depression. Meditation works by breaking the connection between these two responsive regions. It makes it one of the most helpful treatment options to not only treat symptoms of depression. This also helps you reduce it to build a better, more sustainable relationship with your responsiveness to emotions, thoughts, and experiences. Meditation also aids in protecting the hippocampus, which is the part of your brain responsible for memory. It contains gray matter to support memory, and by integrating meditation consistently, increases the gray matter to treat depression directly.

Mindfulness

When depression reaches a point where you feel a deep sense of despair, almost like you have shoveled a deep, dark hole in the sand, and you don't know how to get out of it, then you should intervene. Take a stance. Don't wait for someone to rescue you, because you are stuck in your head to some extent, and if you were able to get there, you could most certainly get yourself out there. Of course, guided support, like going for therapy, regularly, is recommended. Still, at the end of the day, it's all you. Nobody, not even your therapist, will be able to change how you feel. Sure, a professional, or even someone you look up to, will provide you with perspective, making you think and derive solutions. However, you are still the person that has to put in the work.

What is the meaning of mindfulness?

It is defined as a type of meditation where you focus intense awareness of your senses and feelings at the moment, without the presence of interpretation or judgment.

Mindfulness is vital in everything we do, even daily things like eating, studying, working, and many other things. Take eating as an example. If you just eat without thinking about it, you will eat a lot more than you should or eat bad things for you, but you will eat intuitively when you are mindful about eating. You will only eat foods or drink drinks that are good for you and won't overeat. As a result, you are more likely to have a healthier waistline and a more substantial food relation. Just like having a healthy relationship with your diet is necessary for wellness, being mindful of your thoughts and feelings is also required. Because, most of the time, we just react to the things we think and feel. Or, if something happens that we don't like, our first general response is to respond with an upsetting or negative approach to it.

How do you respond when you lose? Do you feel like a loser? Do you think as if you are not good enough or incompetent of doing something? It is a mindless mentality—not one that is focused on growth. It is not one that helps you seek positivity over negativity. Without mindfulness, your approach to life can be rather debilitating, and it can keep you from living your best life. It promotes emotions like feeling out of control or being unbalanced and dissatisfied in all you do, which you want to avoid if you are trying to combat or steer clear depression.

Mindfulness can benefit you by addressing various mental and physical factors such as anxiety, depression, irritable bowel syndrome, fibromyalgia, psoriasis, and post-traumatic stress disorder (PTSD). Mindfulness-based cognitive therapy (MBCT) is a treatment option designed to prevent relapsing in recurrent depression.

Adopting a meditation-mindfulness practice in your life can significantly help you address your health. Suppose you feel like you are physically or mentally affected by altering factors in your life. In that case, you should work to develop a sustainably mindful approach to everything you do. It can help you get rid of the tendency to react negatively, be depressed, or become anxious and feel out of control.

MBCT is effective in preventing recurrent depression. It has been found that it benefits over conditions that involve control by reducing rates of recurrent depression. It also gives comparable benefits to active treatment controls and can be used to achieve similar effects as antidepressants. It is an ideal active treatment control option that is effective for patients struggling with conditions associated with a lack of control. It is best suited for people who have previously suffered from depression and struggle to maintain control over their thoughts and feelings, causing them to relapse.

By adopting mindfulness, you can learn self-control, tolerance, and objectivity. It can promote flexibility, improve concentration, and give you mental clarity. It also exercises your emotional intelligence by allowing you space to stop and think before you react or take your feelings and thoughts seriously. Allowing you a greater sense of perspective teaches you to be kind, accepting, and compassionate with yourself, which seems pretty straightforward. Still, these are all things people lack to feel for themselves. Just like following a balanced diet, mindfulness helps you provide yourself with what you deserve. It promotes satisfaction and self-love, which are both known to be neglected by anyone experiencing depressive symptoms.

If mindfulness can readjust how you feel or think about and treat yourself, it can lay ground rules and prioritize yourself. When you do this, you will be more inclined to look after your mental and emotional wellbeing, both of which are affected by depression. So, reaching this point, the first thing you would want to do is look after yourself and become better. Since you respect yourself, you will do what is necessary to reach this goal.

Muscle Therapy

Therapy involving the muscles is a primary treatment option for depression and the overall treatment of stress in the body. It treats the body as a whole and is considered a musculoskeletal treatment that provides countless benefits for the body and mind. It incorporates rehabilitation stretches and exercises that help to rebalance the body, and in doing so, prevent injuries.

Muscle therapy is a treatment option that uses functional movement techniques. This can be deep tissue massage therapy, myofascial release, trigger point therapy, corrective exercise, or dry needling to remove the body's pain. It can get your body to a point where it can perform at its best. Therapy includes physiotherapy, osteopathic medicine, sports medicine, and chiropractic approaches that allow professional therapists to break down injuries into its simplest form. Once this is established, the right treatment option can be chosen to treat your symptoms' root cause, should you have an injury.

People with injuries, especially severe ones, can feel limited and helpless. They can also feel hopeless. They just want to get back to where they were mentally or physically before an injury occurred. With these feelings, instead of trying to deal with your injury on your own, you should consult a practitioner to have your symptoms treated. Especially when it is accompanied by depression or anxiety.

Muscle therapists often suggest a deep tissue massage to treat deep layers of connective tissue and muscles. This addresses aches and pains, specifically upper back pain, stiff neck, sore shoulders, and leg muscle tightness. Muscle therapy can be helpful in combination with other treatments to treat depression associated with injury or physical impairments.

Tai Chi

Major depressive disorder (MDD) is one of the leading mental illness disorders in the United States. Yet, its current treatment options do not meet the expectations of what patients suffering from MDD needs. Treatment options are accompanied by excessive relapse rates, high non-response rates, and undesirable side effects.

Considering an alternative treatment option, one wouldn't necessarily consider Tai Chi as the treatment option that would cure depression. Still, just like mediation, it delivers incredible results for your brain.

As a mind-body intervention that first originated as a popular martial art, Tai Chi has proven to regulate emotions and relieve mood disorder symptoms. It is also relatively low-intensity, which makes it the perfect exercise body-mind practice for all ages. No matter how immobile you think you are, you can give it a go and improve until you reach a point where it becomes easy to do. Today, Tai Chi is also no longer a practice taught by martial artists in one or two places around town. Due to its popularity, there has been an increased demand for it worldwide and can be easily searched on the internet today to find a range of instructional videos. These videos include simplified and more intensive practices, depending on your skill level.

What makes it so unique and helpful for mind-body connectedness is that it helps you gain control and feel in control of yourself. Suppose you feel in control of what you feel and think. In that case, you will find it easier to resist depression or anything negative associated with it. The effects of Tai Chi have been investigated with the help of clinical trials, one of which examined the impact of depressive symptoms of elderly Chinese patients. The trial included 14 people and found that, after three months of practicing Tai Chi, the patients' depressive symptoms were significantly reduced. It was captured with the help of scoring each of the patients. The decreased scores were considered, along with gender, age, and education.

Social support for each patient was considered and measured by the Lubben Social Network Scale (LSNS), which suggested that it impacted the effects of Tai Chi on the patients' symptoms. The clinical study's outcome suggested some of the first positive and notably successful findings among other clinical trials. Another study conducted measured the practicality and results to treat depressive symptoms with the help of Tai Chi in 39 Chinese U.S. citizens using MDD. The study's outcome suggested that 73% of the patients completed the intervention successfully, which places the effectiveness of Tai Chi as a valuable source to treat depression in a positive light.

Studies found that depression is linked to functional and structural abnormalities in particular regions in the brain related to the processing of emotions, external stimulus, self-representational interactions, and rewards. Tai Chi works in the brain. It modulates these regions and brings balance to networks associated with the feelings of depression in the brain. It suggests that a mind-body intervention like Tai Chi can include attentional, emotion, control, regulation, as well as self-awareness. Brain imaging studies tested for the relevance of the effects of Tai Chi on the brain and body discovered that such intervention studies specifically target the brain region. These include the amygdala, hippocampus, dorsomedial prefrontal cortex, ventromedial prefrontal cortex, and anterior cingulate. The brain regions show that it can be altered to adjust your relationship and responsiveness with depression.

As a result, Tai Chi relieves symptoms of depression. It modulates our inflammation systems and reduces stress. With this, Tai Chi stabilizes the heart rate, decreases salivary cortisol concentrations, and increases noradrenaline excretion in the urine. Additionally, less depressive feelings, tension, fatigue, confusion, anxiety, and anger have been recorded among patients who have consistently taken up Tai Chi over a series of weeks.

NINE

Exercise

Body movement is natural. It's something we all do and do not think of. At times, it can even seem very irrelevant to us until it gets to the point where it becomes restrictive. Exercising indicates moving our bodies beyond just fulfilling daily activities that we often don't consider as movement activity worth talking about. There are many reasons you should add exercise to your daily regime, yet many people don't. It can sometimes seem unnecessary and is something few people view to be a priority. It has also been viewed as an activity we do to get in shape, preferably to lose weight, but this should not be the main reason why we want to exercise.

Moving your body in different ways beyond your daily activities requires maintaining cardiac endurance, strong bones, healthy and mobile muscles, tendons, and joints. Exercise can help you achieve this when you focus on cardiac activity, bodyweight challenges that strengthen your body, and builds mental toughness, strength training, and flexibility. Meditation is also considered an exercise with yoga and Tai Chi being two of the most recognized meditative exercise practices. It is recommended to incorporate various activities into your weekly schedule to gain your mind and body's best possible results. It promotes wellness. Apart from promoting proper functioning of the body and increasing mobility, it changes your mental awareness and your relationship with the ability to decide whether you can or cannot do something.

Building your mental, physical resilience against environmental factors creates a ground of options that are focused on a can-do attitude instead of a hopeless one that is fixated on things it can't control.

Exercise may seem like something that doesn't contribute to the ability to make better and more growth-oriented decisions for yourself. Still, it does indeed alter the way you think and perceive difficult situations. If you can overcome an exercise routine when you are unfit or feel like you can't do it, then you create the idea in your mind that you are capable of more than your thoughts tell you that you are. Every time you overcome a challenging workout, your brain gets presented with the idea that you can do something. The more you push yourself, the more it adopts the analogy to control your decisions, thoughts, and feelings.

Approaching exercise and building mental toughness to commit to an exercise routine can help you take action to make decisions. You can see them through, rather than choosing to disappoint yourself. If you can start keeping yourself accountable, you can become disciplined. This could aid in the control you have over your emotions and reactiveness to things that are hindering or negatively affecting you. By controlling how you respond, you can take control of your feelings and manage bad thoughts by replacing them with good ones. Since exercise also releases endorphins in the brain, it can instantly improve your mood and provide you with new energy. It is something no medication or therapy can do on the spot. When you complete an exercise or physical activity session, you will likely have mental clarity and perspective. It can cause you to focus on positivity without giving negativity a single thought. Exercise helps us get rid of our frustration, and can help you overcome feelings of anger, sadness, anguish, and all that is related to stress. It can tackle anxiety and make you feel in control of something that will establish stability in your life. Once you feel in control, your tendency to fall into depression or feel like you aren't able to address things in your life will go away.

Given that exercise has many other health benefits, like lowering your blood pressure, protecting against diabetes and heart disease, and improving sleep, it will improve your health and aid in your journey to achieve complete wellness. Depression is known for causing health issues, whether diagnosed by your doctor or displayed in symptoms only recognized by you. In this case, if you can integrate exercise into your daily regime, even if it's just 20 minutes a day, you can immediately improve your health. Besides, apart from the endless bottle of benefits, when you look good, you feel good.

So, if this is the case, why don't people walk, run, or workout with a YouTube video? Because, in reality, you do not have to spend money today to exercise. Well, first, you need to overcome any potential mental barriers you may have. Some people can start exercising without hesitation in their minds. They usually don't even consider not working out, while most people are the opposite. With exercise, the majority will always find an excuse as to why they do not have to do it, and as a result, postpone it. It happens when exercise is not a priority. So if you are serious about making a difference and take control of your life, whatever will make you feel good, including eating a balanced diet, prioritize it.

Depression holds us back from doing too many things that are good for us. It keeps us in our comfort zone, disrupts sleep, and messes with our appetite. As well as increasing pain perception, reducing energy, and cause more body aches than we have. Know this, the point of starting an exercise routine is the hardest part of actually doing it. When you decide to commit to exercise, make sure you find something that will keep you motivated. Opting for something you genuinely like, an enjoyable exercise type, will surely keep you interested in maintaining a workout schedule. Once you see physical and mental results, it will be relatively easy to keep coming back for more.

TEN

Eat a Balanced Diet
_____

IF YOU SUFFER FROM DEPRESSION, YOU CAN IMAGINE HOW IT affects your relationship with food. In most cases, it can be the first line of comfort people seek. In other cases, not looking after yourself by eating a balanced diet or eating enough to sustain your body can also be an option for people suffering from depression. Eating too much or not eating enough at all can seem like a coping mechanism for depression. Since food is always there for you, it is easy to turn to it as a means of comfort. In the same way, not eating can seem like a form of punishment or self-expression of your feelings.

Depending on how bad your depression and anxiety are, it could swing either way. It's quite surprising to think that the average individual, depressed or not depressed has a bad relationship with food. Food is your friend. It is not supposed to comfort you, and you're not supposed to feel bad when you eat something unhealthy or when you eat enough. It's there to provide nutrients for your body, sustain your organs and necessary functions of your body, and provide you with energy to perform at your best. Eating a balanced diet can help you treat depression. Even though food is not considered a treatment option that will help you fight depression, eating the right foods can make you feel good.

When you do not eat enough food or skip a meal, you will notice that you feel like you don't have the energy or rather be lazy than constructive. Still, when you look after yourself, this changes. You feel like you are equipped and energized to face the day. When you visit your doctor and therapist, they will advise you to follow a balanced diet filled with nutrient-rich foods. It will be accompanied by an exercise routine as a part of your treatment plan.

Foods to Prioritize To Eat a Balanced Diet

Antioxidant-Rich Foods

Foods that contain plenty of antioxidants are generally fresh produce or what we recognize today as super foods. You wouldn't imagine that the body could make damaging molecules that negatively affect our cells, yet it does. It creates free radicals that cause cell damage, aging, along with many other problems. It can also weaken the immune system and place our brain at risk. Since there is no way to stop free radicals from being created in the body, it's necessary to address them with food. You can reduce the destructive effects thereof by adding antioxidant-rich foods to your diet. These include:

Beta-Carotene

Food such as apricots, peaches, cantaloupe, broccoli, spinach, sweet potato, pumpkin, carrots, and collards.

Vitamin C

Oranges, grapefruit, kiwi, blueberries, strawberries, tomato, broccoli, peppers, and potatoes are chocked full of Vitamin C.

Vitamin E

Vegetable oils, margarine, nuts, seeds, and wheat germ all contain Vitamin E.

Protein-Rich Foods

Our bodies require protein-rich foods to repair existing and build new tissues. It is also necessary to make hormones, enzymes, and body chemicals, build bones, cartilage, skin, muscles, and blood. Protein can be found in foods that are either good or bad for you, which is why you should be mindful of adding only good sources of protein to your diet. It includes chicken, tuna, salmon, turkey, lean beef, beans, peas, low-fat cheese, milk, yogurt, poultry, and soy products. Some of these good protein sources, like chicken, tuna, and turkey contain the amino acid, tryptophan, which helps the body; make the good feeling hormone, serotonin. By adding healthy protein sources to your daily diet, preferably one serving per meal, you can promote weight-loss. You can keep your body's health in tip-top shape and boost energy levels.

Mediterranean Diet Foods

As one of the most popular diets for eating a healthy and balanced diet, foods from the Mediterranean diet is the most recommended diet for people suffering from depression. That's because it is filled with foods that contain folate and vitamin B12—both of which are nutrients that treat depression. It includes legumes, fruits, nuts, dark green vegetables, and low-fat animal products that are high in vitamin B12 and folate.

Smart Carbohydrates

As one of the most judged food sources, carbohydrates have received a somewhat good and bad name for themselves. For decades, we have been taught to reduce carbs' intake or cut it out altogether if we want to lose weight or become healthier. However, carbohydrates are significant and form a big part of what makes a balanced diet, just like its other badly-perceived scrutinized neighbor, fats. Carbohydrates are linked to a mood-boosting brain chemical, serotonin. Carbohydrate cravings have been linked to low serotonin levels, which means the type of carbs you eat is essential. Our bodies reject some carbohydrates while it welcomes others. It does not process sugary foods or carb-rich foods efficiently. Instead, it deposits it as fat stores. Complex carbohydrates like whole-grain foods, on the other hand, are recommended to eat a healthy, balanced diet. It includes fruits, vegetables, and legumes like beans, lentils, and peas, all of which are rich in fiber.

Vitamin D-Rich Foods

We all know that the sun contains vitamin D, so if you don't want to get your vitamin D in food, you can get your daily dose by catching some sun. Just 10 minutes of direct exposure to sunlight can give you the vitamin D you need to feel good. Apart from standard depression, one can also get seasonal depression due to a lack of vitamin D from sunlight. The weather can affect your mood directly. During winter and autumn months, it's necessary to eat foods that are rich in vitamin D. Food such as fatty fish, vitamin-D fortified foods, beef liver, cheese, and egg yolks. They will make up for the lack of sunlight.

Selenium-Rich Foods

Selenium is a mineral that supports the adequate functioning of different body parts. It protects the body against cognitive decline, thyroid issues, and asthma. There is a link between a lack of this powerful mineral and a poor mood, so getting the daily recommended amount of 55 mg for adults per day, is necessary. Selenium is often prescribed as a supplement for patients diagnosed with depression to help maintain and recover the condition's symptoms. However, before doctors generally prescribe selenium supplements, they recommend you adjust your diet. With anything, it's always better to retrieve vitamins and minerals from natural sources. Selenium-rich foods include lean meat, beans, legumes, low-fat dairy products, whole grains products, seafood, nuts, and seeds.

Omega-3 Fatty Acids

When you hear the word omega-3 or essential fatty acids,

you know it's something meant to be used for your brain's proper and healthy functioning. Omega-3 can be found in fatty fish like salmon, mackerel, sardines, tuna, shad, and anchovies, which are some of the richest sources of these fatty acids. You can also find it in nuts, particularly walnuts, flaxseed, canola and soybean oil, and dark green or leafy vegetables like spinach, kale, Swiss chard, and rocket. These foods, or a supplement—usually a fish oil supplement—are recommended to treat higher depression rates. People who don't eat fish regularly are more likely to suffer from depression than those who do. Since it's also good for proper heart and brain functioning, you should make a point of incorporating it into your diet. If you suffer from depression, adding two to three good fish sources into your diet a week and four to five sources of other omega-3 fatty acids a week can only help treat your condition.

ELEVEN

Avoid Alcohol and Recreational Drugs

THE CHEMICALS IN YOUR BRAIN ARE BALANCED. THEY ARE AT A level of what they should be to work in sync for you to function optimally. With depression, your brain's chemicals get altered, as does it when using drugs and alcohol. It doesn't only change the way your brain works, but also how your body functions. Alcohol and drugs alter your brain's chemistry, responsible for thinking, feeling, and creating decisions. Although you may be aware of this, with depression, it's not so easy to comply with the rules. When you have depression, especially a severe case thereof, it can feel like you want to get rid of the way you feel. As your feelings may be accompanied by pain, getting rid of them with alcohol and drugs can seem very tempting.

People who take medication for depression or anxiety are not allowed to drink alcohol or use recreational drugs, as it will only make an existing problem worse. In essence, it's not recommended for anyone to use these substances, which are prone to fall into negative feelings or experience pain through their emotions. Any thought or feeling that alters your judgment should be a direct indication that you shouldn't be reckless with addictive substances. Whether you have been clinically diagnosed with depression or not. Even if you don't feel like substances will harm you, you will know whether it negatively affects you if you are honest with yourself. With that, you should follow the responsible decision to steer clear of them.

It's nearly impossible to predict your response to them by affecting chemical messaging processes in the brain. With the use of illegal drugs, you run the risk of not knowing what is in them. You may have it in your mind that they will make everything better, but they will leave you feeling even worse than before. You can experience feelings of anxiety, agitation, feel unmotivated, moody, and approach everything without feeling in control. It can also affect your reality and make things appear worse than they are, contributing to depression. Although using alcohol and drugs seem like a short-term fix that won't affect you, know that it will. Addiction is recognized as a serious problem for a reason. It is as serious as the illness itself and requires professional advice and treatment. Being intoxicated can make you do things that are entirely out of character. You may catch yourself behaving in ways you never thought were possible. Since you're not in control of what you do under the influence, you run the risk of causing trouble in your relationships, work, and home.

Suppose you have existing drug or alcohol habits. In that case, especially if they have already progressed to the point of addiction, it will be difficult to change these habits. Depression and anxiety make you feel out of control, and as a result, clouds your judgment. To address addiction or the potential thereof, you should seek support. Only with this and perseverance will you make positive alterations in your physical and mental well-being.

There are three primary types of drugs: depressants, hallucinogens, and depressants, making the body and mind react differently.

Types of Drugs and Recreational Drugs to Avoid

Depressants

These recreational drugs are known to slow down your body, breathing, and heart rate. It can cause you to experience vomiting and nausea, impair your ability to think clearly and be unaware of what is happening around you. Depressants are often recognized as antidepressants only. On the contrary, they include alcohol, cannabis, heroin, sedatives, and inhalants. These are all addictive depressants that can seem like a short-term fix that causes you to feel good momentarily. This temporary feeling of improvement can also be addictive and usually makes people return to their drug of choice. Depression can get so bad that it makes you feel like you want to feel good, even if it's for a short period, which is quite dangerous. It's what causes one to act impulsively and take risks.

Stimulants

You can seriously harm your body by trying to speed up the process of muscle growth or fitness performance. Stimulants like steroids and methamphetamines—cocaine and ecstasy—are used to speed your body up unnaturally. Increase your heart rate, blood pressure, and body temperature. People often resort to using stimulants because it makes them feel like they have confidence; energy, motivation, and can decrease their need for sleep. However, if this is brought on by a drug, it's not right for you. It can cause you to become paranoid, agitated, anxious, aggressive, and even violent. It can also cause physical side effects like headaches, stomach cramps, and dizziness.

Cannabis

Known as a drug that aids in relaxation, which is why so many people use it, cannabis can cause panic attacks, anxiety, paranoia, and yes, depression. It's hard to believe that something that seems so harmless can make you feel bad, but it does. Even so, it's not usually talked about. It may also shock you to learn that cannabis doesn't only cause these side effects in people with mental health conditions. It also causes it in those who don't and can ignite something serious, like depression, in someone that hasn't experienced it before.

Hallucinogens

Drugs that affect your idea of time, the state of your emotional well-being, and cause you to experience auditory and visual hallucinations. It can also alter your reality and cause you to see things that are not there, indicating symptoms similar to Schizophrenia. Apart from taking drugs to bring on the effects of making you feel like you can escape from your circumstances, the results can also cause flashbacks that are disturbing to you, especially with hallucinogen as ketamine, LSD, and magic mushrooms.

As a non-recreational drug, smoking cigarettes can be just as harmful as other addictions, particularly when you are so attached to it that it seems impossible to quit. Many people start smoking because they are depressed and do it as a means of deliberate self-harm. However, it can make your depression worse. Since quitting smoking is the best thing you can do for your health it's best to avoid it altogether if you are diagnosed with or think you have depression. It can also improve your mental well-being.

How Do You Know If A Recreational Drug Is Bad For You?

You have to consider whether it boosts your mood fast or gradually and whether it is temporary or permanent. With this, you will know what is right and what is bad for you. Regular depressants can alter your mood to a shallow point that can cause you to think unclearly and resort to self-harm or suicide. This is a serious reason to abstain from alcohol and drugs.

TWELVE

Spend Time Relaxing

MAJOR DEPRESSIVE DISORDER (MDD) HAS THE POWER TO impact your emotional and physical well-being. Its symptoms can be displayed with a poor appetite, lack of concentration, persistent sadness, low energy, feelings of constant tiredness or hopelessness, and the presence of suicidal thoughts. Depression is an ongoing battle, one that seems like it controls your life, but in reality, it doesn't. When you break it down into smaller parts than what you have in your mind, it becomes more bearable—even if it's only slightly.

When it occurs, it's for a reason, which can range from either being random feelings of sadness or be caused by genetics - something you can't cure. In this case, you have to learn how to live with it the best way you can. You have to make depression work for you and adjust yourself, including your habits and address your triggers, to deal with it successfully. Whatever makes you feel worse should also be addressed as an issue for concern. If you can get a handle on your symptoms, living with depression won't seem as bad as it feels in the moment of experiencing it.

Given that it not only affects your mental well-being but your emotional well-being as well. One thing you can do is look after your physical health as much as you can. By doing this, you are showing yourself that you can control at least one thing necessary, your physical health, which will help your journey solve issues related to mental health and emotional well-being.

Taking care of your physical health means not only to review your habits, eat a clean, balanced diet, or exercise. It also means spending enough time recharging. Relaxing helps fight depression as it is a form of self-care. When we relax, our body's blood flow changes and provides us with more energy, making us calmer by presenting us with a clearer, concise mind. It allows us to make better decisions and maintain a positive perspective, promoting the development of new ideas and positive thoughts that improve concentration, memory, and ability to process the things that affect us the most deeply. When we relax, our heart rate also slows down. It reduces our blood pressure naturally, which promotes our physical health. It also naturally calms the mind and relieves tension in the entire body.

By spending more time relaxing, we stop fixating on the things we cannot control. As this is one of the leading causes of depression, we relieve our minds from one of the leading causes of depression. When we stop fixating on things that are out of our control, we shift our thoughts to the things that are real and happening in the present time, and with this, reduce feelings of being out of control. Then, we also gain control over our emotions. Relaxing can aid in the relationship we have with ourselves. It can make us gain respect for how we feel, increase our self-worth, and motivate us to take care of ourselves first. If you think about the deraling effects of depression on self-image, care, and worth, it can transcend everything. It helps us develop a sense of importance, which is very important for recovering from depression.

Take a Bath

It may seem more efficient to take a shower to save time. Still, considering relaxation, it's all about taking the time that you don't usually have. Even taking a bath every day is not something you should be feeling guilty about. Especially after a long day at work or if you have a lot of home responsibilities, like cooking, cleaning, and raising kids. Or both! Shout out to the super moms and dads, who manage to do it all and still stay sane. At the end of a long day, or if you are taking a day off for yourself, taking a long, hot bath is just the thing that will help you unwind your mind. It can relieve tension from the body, and since there isn't much to do but think, make you feel good and think clearly about the things inside your mind. Since you have time to yourself without any interruptions, it's also great for planning the next day in your mind, or not thinking of anything at all.

Taking a bath is not just something we get recommended because of its potential relaxing benefits. No. Instead, it is referred to as hydrotherapy, which uses both hot and cold water to achieve beneficial effects for the body. Taking ice-cold baths, which seems dreadful, can have benefits for your body too. Today, it's called cryotherapy—the practice of taking ice baths to reduce muscle strain, usually a regular training for athletes like runners after a big event.

While not everybody is up for an ice bath, hydrotherapy can benefit you in the following ways:

- Improve heart health only by combining hot and cold water. Bathing in excessively hot water has been linked to damaging the heart, particularly in people with pre-existing heart conditions. Warm baths can still be good for your heart by making it beat faster, but you should ensure it is not too hot and avoid it if you have a heart condition.
- Helps you breathe easier. When water goes beyond your chest with your head still outside of the water, it can influence

your lung capacity and increase oxygen intake. It is due to the water's temperature and pressure, which both affect the chest and lungs.

- Improves brain and nervous system functioning. Being submerged in water reduces pain and inflammation. It also calms the nervous system, reduces anxiety and stress in the body, and boosts a positive mood. It can relieve pain in people with multiple sclerosis and pain associated with discomfort in the entire body. Its calming affects aids in a healthier mind-body connection.
- Provides low impact resistance for muscles, bones, and joints. When your body gets used to working against low impact resistance, it can aid in stronger muscles, bones, and joints, which reduces your risk of injury.
- Cares for skin, hair, and eyes. Fluid, in combination with steaming, provides proper hydration for the body. Soaking in water with bath salts or in the presence of aromatherapy in the bathroom while you take a bath can enhance relaxation in the body. It creates a sense of self-care that also feels good.

Watch Television

Sitting in front of the television is not something the modern generation usually gets encouraged to do. Sitting down and watching TV does stimulate your brain healthily. It places it in a state similar to meditation. Watching TV is not just what we resort to when we are bored. It helps to calm you down and relieves feelings related to agitation. Of course, it's never recommended to sit down indoors and watch television for hours. Still, you can spend one to two hours a day or every other day relaxing your mind. When you watch something you like, it's also a bonus, because you are taking the time to entertain yourself and care for yourself. By putting yourself first in this way, you are also practicing self-care. Something which is neglected when we spend most of our time working or paying attention to stress and responsibilities.

TV can become an addiction because it releases good feeling chemicals in the brain, called endorphins. It has a similar effect on the brain as morphine, which you can imagine is highly addictive. In this case, in combination with discipline, television is a suitable relaxation method you can implement daily for a short period or a few times a week for more extended periods.

Spend Time Outside

While television is preferred by many people today, spending more time outdoors aids in a healthier and clearer mind. When you are outside, you are exposed to fresh air and the elements of nature, which benefits your mental health. It can also be beneficial for people with mental illnesses by relieving depression, stress, and anxiety. This is due to the positive, stress less effect nature has on our health. It's usually quiet or filled with relaxing and tranquil noises. Due to adequate relaxation, it improves one's mood immediately. It reduces negative emotions by shifting your focus on things that worry you, including feelings of irritability. It can also calm the body to the extent of relieving insomnia, headaches, indigestion, and tension in the body.

It also has other mental benefits. It benefits the brain and aids in therapeutic properties, improves feelings, increases energy, and focus. It can reduce ADHD symptoms, improve creative thinking, and restore your brain's capacity to be more attentive. Spending more time outside isn't as easy for people who live in cities, but when possible, start with going for a hike on a hill or taking a walk in a park or woods. You can take your workout outside by walking, jogging, cycling, and jogging too. If you are stuck in the city, you can also book a weekend away or drive out to a nature reserve or public park, or book a camping trip.

Take Up Gardening

Gardening is known for relieving stress successfully. While many people may be hesitant to give it a try as they don't like to get their hands dirty or perceive it as a waste of time, it's good for you. Not only does it present you with an opportunity to spend more time outdoors, but it also calms your mind. When you take it up on a sunny day, you will be in for some vitamin D too, which naturally boosts your mood. Gardening is recognized as more effective for reducing stress than reading books.

If you think about the relaxing effect reading a book has on your mind and body, allowing yourself to escape reality or gain clarity, you can understand why having a green thumb can indeed be very good for you. When you are outside, you are less prone to thinking about bad things, that is also why it is recommended to spend more time outdoors than indoors. If you want to be constructive while gardening, you can grow a vegetable garden or find suitable plants for the environment or provide health benefits. Some plants include herbs, Aloe Vera, and the spekboom, which filters carbon dioxide and puts oxygen back into the atmosphere.

Read a Book

There is a misconception about the new way of reading, which is on a smartphone, computer, or tablet, popularized in recent years as the Kindle. E-reading, though, has a different effect on the brain than physically holding a hard copied book in your hands and reading it. It's proven that reading helps you reduce anxiety and stress. It's very simple to do. As a result, people often don't make the most of it, especially in a technology-driven world.

Is everything available on the internet for us to search and read there? Yes, it is, but if you want to relax, looking for something to read online can worsen your stress of everyday life. That's because we are prone to look at everything that seems even remotely interesting online. We scroll and scroll and click on things that, for the most part, are negative, which is bad for us.

Opening a book has a unique effect on the body because when you pick up a book and open it to hold in your hands, you are committing yourself to relax. Something we can't say the same for when we are reading online. The literary world can distract us by keeping us captivated in what we read. It has also been proven to relieve tension in the body's muscles by a study conducted in 2009 by the University of Sussex. They found that reading reduces stress by 68%, which means it works much faster than most other relaxation methods, including music or drinking tea. This makes sense as you can get lost in another world and completely forget about your reality and responsibilities during the time you read. (University of Minnesota, 2009)

If you are interested to start reading and tackling your stress and anxiety, consider this:

- The type of book you choose doesn't have to be on the best-seller list. It can be anything welcoming to your mind, whether it's fiction or nonfiction.
- Reading reduces stress only when you pick up something you enjoy. Reading something that upsets you even slightly will not have a positive effect on your stress levels and will make you struggle to relax.
- When reading, consider how you feel each time after reading for a while. We don't always consider how relaxing activities make us feel. Still, if you recognize its benefits, you'll

return to it as a coping mechanism for your worries. This can also help you cope with depression.

Saying "No" to Unnecessary Commitments

Being a people pleaser can seem like a harmless thing, but it messes with you emotionally and mentally in truth. It can cause resentment or feelings of unpleasantness because when you frequently say yes to something you don't want to do or don't like, you sort of go against yourself. It is not a nice feeling, and it's one that introverts particularly, experience a lot. Sometimes, it feels like you have to say yes. Perhaps because you are a people pleaser and you would like to keep everybody around you happy, but maybe not. Anyone reserved, quiet, or introverted may feel forced to say yes to do things they don't want to do. It's an honest lie to an extent. You tell someone you will do something because you want to do it, but that's not the truth. You only tell someone that you will do it because you want to keep the peace, or even worse, feel included. Some even feel like they have to prove something, especially the case in teenagers and young adults.

Saying no is not bad, and this is not made clear to us when we grow up. When you reject an offer or invitation, you show the world you respect who you are and what you want. It is not selfish. It's courageous and inspiring, to the right people. What you should know is that not everyone is the right person for you, and you shouldn't feel forced to adjust yourself to what others need. By being yourself, you are displaying self-respect, and in all honesty, you can conquer anything with this. If you only do things you like or want to do—something that excites and impassion you—you will feel good. You will appreciate that you live according to your standards, which is a blessing unaccompanied by stress.

THIRTEEN

Get Enough Sleep

WE SPEND NEARLY A THIRD OF OUR LIVES ASLEEP, WHICH SEEMS ridiculous if you think how short life is, right? However, without adequate sleep, we cannot live our best life. Sleep is as crucial for your body as drinking water, eating food, and breathing. When you consider this, it makes a lot more sense to get seven to eight hours of sleep each night than scrolling endlessly through social media feeds online or watching Netflix till the early hours of the morning. Sleeping helps our bodies recover mentally and physically, which is required after exerting energy every day.

When we exercise, we automatically sleep better because our body needs to recover from excessive activity. Sleeping enough and developing a pattern that supports your daily energy needs also promotes feeling better and improves mental health. It makes us less inclined to be emotional and reduces our mental reaction to negative feelings. It also promotes a healthier body as sleeping efficient hours encourage weight-loss.

Getting your body to a point where it can sleep soundly is one of the best things you can do for your body. Since it makes you feel OK, not sluggish, and anxious like a lack of sleep, you can feel like you can conquer your day and achieve more than you would've otherwise. With stress comes the immense struggle of suffering from insomnia, bad dreams, and discomfort to fall asleep. This is why we should align different elements to create the perfect space for sleeping soundly.

To Improve Your Sleep

Sleep and Rise At the Same Time Daily

Don't say you can't do it. Just like anything, if you want to achieve the benefits of sleep, you can do it. By adjusting your schedule a little, you can make it happen. It, of course, requires discipline and prioritizing sleep accordingly, which is what you should do. You give a little, and you receive a lot of benefits. Now, just because you should stick to a schedule to regulate your sleep pattern does not mean you have to go to bed early. You can fall asleep at 11 p.m. every night and wake up at 7 a.m. Just be sure not to press the snooze button because you don't want to get too much sleep either.

Don't Get Too Much Sleep

You may think the more you sleep, the better you will feel, or if you haven't been sleeping much in the week, that you can make up for it over the weekends. However, sleeping less than six hours a night consistently, and then sleeping more than nine hours once or twice a week is very bad for you. It sends mixed signals to your brain and has been linked to higher stress levels and weight gain. It also decreases energy, promotes fatigue, disrupts your emotions, and impairs your memory.

No Screens Before Bed

It's a habit for pretty much everybody today to look at their phones before they go to sleep, and sometimes, scroll for hours or watch TV right before they go to sleep. It disrupts sleep and promotes insomnia by keeping the mind too busy to switch off. Before bed, you should take at least an hour to relax and stop thinking. Since bright lights, like those on smartphones, makes your brain think it's time, it's also quite bad for falling asleep.

Don't Eat Before Bed

Eating before bed keeps your body's digestive system going, which is not good if you're trying to fall asleep. That's why you shouldn't eat at least three hours before bed.

Conclusion

To fight depression takes an act of resilience. Even if you don't think you possess the strength to, first of all, admit that you have depression and then treat it, you have to convince yourself that you do. Without thinking about how bad your condition is or how terrible you feel when experiencing thoughts and feelings that seem out of control, know this. They are your thoughts and feelings, and when you set them aside to think clearly about everything, you will realize why you have to fight it.

Thinking about what depression does to your life and how derailing it can be, is reason enough to scrape together the strength you have and address it. By doing so, you prove a point to yourself that you can take charge of your life and be a person that is in control rather than controlled by something inside you. Life will always respond to you, but that doesn't matter. What matters is what you do with it and how you deal with it. That is the true definition of overcoming something beyond what you or others can see. It's your depression, it's your anxiety, but it's also your mind. You can control it. You have to say yes to it. Value yourself enough to take care of yourself, feel good about yourself, and, if necessary, get help.

Conclusion

The most challenging part of it all is starting. Once you see how good it feels to take control of your life, it will become second nature as something you want to commit to. If you're going to live your best life, the outcome of the journey you choose is up to you.

References

20 Divorce Facts for 2020. (2019, January 7). GillespieShields. https://gillespieshields.com/20-divorce-facts-for-2020/

Ackerman, C. E. (2020, January 9). 83 Benefits of Journaling for Depression, Anxiety, and Stress. PositivePsychology.Com. https://positivepsychology.com/benefits-of-journaling/

Bayes-Fleming, N. (2018, September 28). Using Mindfulness to Treat Depression - Mindful. Mindful. https://www.mindful.org/using-mindfulness-to-treat-depression/

Clarke, J. (2020, May 11). Which Foods Can Help Fight Depression? (S. Gans (Ed.)). Verywell Mind. https://www.verywellmind.com/foods-for-depression-4156403

Depression: A Mind/Body Connection. (n.d.). WebMD; WebMD https://www.webmd.com/depression/video/depression-a-mind-body-connection

Depression and Diet. (n.d.). WebMD; WebMD. https://www.webmd.com/depression/guide/diet-recovery#1

Depression red flags: when to see your doctor - Mental Health - MedBroadcast.com. (n.d.). Www.Medbroadcast.Com. https://www.medbroadcast.com/channel/mental-health/depression/depression-red-flags-when-to-see-your-doctor

Drugs, alcohol and mental health. (n.d.). Beyondblue.Org.Au; beyondblue. https://www.beyondblue.org.au/the-facts/drugs-alcohol-and-mental-health

familydoctor.org editorial staff. (2019, July 22). Mind/Body Connection: How Emotions Affect Health. Familydoctor.Org. https://familydoctor.org/mindbody-connection-how-your-emotions-affect-your-health/

Harvard Health Publishing. (2013, July). Exercise is an all-natural treatment to fight depression - Harvard Health. Harvard Health; Harvard Health. https://www.health.harvard.edu/mind-and-mood/exercise-is-an-all-natural-treatment-to-fight-depression

Harvard Health Publishing. (2018, August). How meditation helps with depression - Harvard Health. Harvard Health; Harvard Health. https://www.health.harvard.edu/mind-and-mood/how-meditation-helps-with-depression

Higuera, V. (2020, August 17). Finding Ways to Relax and Recharge with MDD. Healthline. https://www.healthline.com/health/depression/managing-major-depressive-disorder/relax-recharge#1

Holland, K. (2018, February 11). Depression: Types, Causes, Treatment, and More. Healthline. https://www.healthline.com/health/depression

Holland, K. (2018, May 14). Acupuncture for Depression: Does It Really Work? And 12 Other FAQs. Healthline. https://www.healthline.com/health/depression/acupuncture-for-depression

How to look after your mental health. (n.d.). Mental Health Foundation. https://www.mentalhealth.org.uk/publications/how-to-mental-health

Kara Mayer Robinson. (n.d.). How Writing in a Journal Helps Manage Depression. WebMD; WebMD.

References

https://www.webmd.com/depression/features/writing-your-way-out-of-depression#1

Kong, J., Wilson, G., Park, J., Pereira, K., Walpole, C., & Yeung, A. (2019). Treating Depression With Tai Chi: State of the Art and Future Perspectives. Frontiers in Psychiatry, 10. https://doi.org/10.3389/fpsyt.2019.00237

Krans, B. (2019, April 1). Massage Therapy for Depression. Healthline; Healthline Media. https://www.healthline.com/health/depression/massage-therapy

Mayo Clinic Staff. (n.d.). Stress relief: When and how to say no. Mayo Clinic. https://www.mayoclinic.org/healthy-lifestyle/stress-management/in-depth/stress-relief/art-20044494

Melgar, L. (2019, May 17). Are School Shootings Becoming More Frequent? We Ran The Numbers. KUNC. https://www.kunc.org/2019-05-17/are-school-shootings-becoming-more-frequent-we-ran-the-numbers

Morin, A. (2018, May 9). The Beginner's Guide to Changing Negative Thoughts. Psychology Today. https://www.psychologytoday.com/za/blog/what-mentally-strong-people-dont-do/201805/the-beginners-guide-changing-negative-thoughts

Ontario Parks. (2020, January 29). Mental health benefits of spending time in nature. Parks Blog. https://www.ontarioparks.com/parksblog/mental-health-benefits-outdoors/

Optimal Health Manifesto - How To Live Your Best Life. (2018, April 19). The Wellness Connection. https://thewellnessconnection.com/optimal-health-manifesto/

O'Sullivan, C. (2016, September 19). The importance of sleep. Mental Health Foundation. https://www.mentalhealth.org.uk/blog/importance-sleep

Parekh, R., & Givon, L. (2019, January). What is Psychotherapy? Psychiatry.Org. https://www.psychiatry.org/patients-families/psychotherapy

Penman, D. (2011, October 14). Curing Depression with

References

Mindfulness Meditation. Psychology Today. https://www.psychologytoday.com/intl/blog/mindfulness-in-frantic-world/201110/curing-depression-mindfulness-meditation

Pentucket Medical. (2018, September 4). 10 Scientifically Proven Health Benefits of Taking a Bath | Pentucket Medical. Pentucket Medical. https://pmaonline.com/posts/adult-primary-care/10-scientifically-proven-health-benefits-of-taking-a-bath/

Powell, A. (2018, April 19). How Mindfulness May Change the Brain in Depressed Patients - Mindful. Mindful. https://www.mindful.org/how-mindfulness-may-change-the-brain-in-depressed-patients/

Psychotherapy & Depression. (2018, February 2). Cleveland Clinic. https://my.clevelandclinic.org/health/treatments/9300--psychotherapy-for-depression

Raypole, C. (2019, May 29). How to Help a Depressed Friend. Healthline; Healthline Media. https://www.healthline.com/health/how-to-help-a-depressed-friend

Reading for Stress Relief | Taking Charge of Your Health & Wellbeing. (n.d.). Taking Charge of Your Health & Wellbeing. https://www.takingcharge.csh.umn.edu/reading-stress-relief

Riopel, L. (2019, January 9). Goal Setting in Counseling and Therapy (Incl. Workbooks & Templates). PositivePsychology.Com. https://positivepsychology.com/goal-setting-counseling-therapy/

Schimelpfening, N. (2020, March 24). Types of Psychotherapy for Depression (S. Gans (Ed.)). Verywell Mind; Verywellmind. https://www.verywellmind.com/types-of-psychotherapy-for-depression-1067407

Tom, T. (2011, July 9). Teacher Tom: Watching Television Is Relaxing. Teacher Tom. http://teachertomsblog.blogspot.com/2011/07/watching-television-is-relaxing.html

Watson, L. R., Fraser, M., & Ballas, P. (2019). Journaling for Mental Health - Health Encyclopedia - University of

References

Rochester Medical Center. Rochester.Edu. https://www.urmc.rochester.edu/encyclopedia/content.aspx?ContentID=4552&ContentTypeID=1

What causes depression. (n.d.). Beyondblue.Org.Au; beyondblue. https://www.beyondblue.org.au/the-facts/depression/what-causes-depression

What Is Depression? (n.d.). WebMD; WebMD. https://www.webmd.com/depression/guide/what-is-depression#1

What is Muscle Therapy? (n.d.). Muscletherapy. https://www.muscletherapyaustralia.com.au/what-is-muscle-therapy

Who can I talk to about my depression? (n.d.). MHA Screening - Mental Health America. https://screening.mhanational.org/content/who-can-i-talk-about-my-depression

Xiong, G. (2018, October 5). Why It's Important to Care for Your Mental Health. Medium; Doctor On Demand. https://blog.doctorondemand.com/why-its-important-to-care-for-your-mental-health-834c8670b889

About the Author

Monique Joiner Siedlak is a writer, witch, and warrior on a mission to awaken people to their greatest potential through the power of storytelling infused with mysticism, modern paganism, and new age spirituality. At the young age of 12, she began rigorously studying the fascinating philosophy of Wicca. By the time she was 20, she was self-initiated into the craft, and hasn't looked back ever since. To this day, she has authored over 40 books pertaining to the magick and mysteries of life.

To find out more about Monique Joiner Siedlak artistically, spiritually, and personally, feel free to visit her **official website**.

www.mojosiedlak.com

facebook.com/mojosiedlak
twitter.com/mojosiedlak
instagram.com/mojosiedlak
pinterest.com/mojosiedlak
bookbub.com/authors/monique-joiner-siedlak

More Books by Monique Joiner Siedlak

Practical Magick
Wiccan Basics
Candle Magick
Wiccan Spells
Love Spells
Abundance Spells
Herb Magick
Moon Magick
Creating Your Own Spells
Gypsy Magic
Protection Magick
Celtic Magick
Shamanic Magick

African Magic
Hoodoo
Seven African Powers: The Orishas
Cooking for the Orishas
Lucumi: The Ways of Santeria
Voodoo of Louisiana
Haitian Vodou

Orishas of Trinidad
Connecting with your Ancestors

The Yoga Collective
Yoga for Beginners
Yoga for Stress
Yoga for Back Pain
Yoga for Weight Loss
Yoga for Flexibility
Yoga for Advanced Beginners
Yoga for Fitness
Yoga for Runners
Yoga for Energy
Yoga for Your Sex Life
Yoga: To Beat Depression and Anxiety
Yoga for Menstruation
Yoga to Detox Your Body
Yoga to Tone Your Body

A Natural Beautiful You
Creating Your Own Body Butter
Creating Your Own Body Scrub
Creating Your Own Body Spray

Last Chance Join My Newsletter!

If you missed it, I have a free gift available for you and wanted to remind you it's still available.

mojosiedlak.com/self-help-and-yoga-newsletter

Thank you for reading my book.
I really appreciate all your feedback and would love to hear what you have to say! Please leave your review at your favorite retailer!

www.ingramcontent.com/pod-product-compliance
Lightning Source LLC
Chambersburg PA
CBHW071309060426
42444CB00034B/1744